Enjoy +

Phone 284-3128

Onion Avenue

A novel by

Nora Stangland McNab

PLEASE RETURN THIS BOOK TO Seniorfit for our Book EXchange —

thanx
Sharon

International Standard Book Number: 0-942323-14-9

Published by
North American Heritage Press
A DIVISION OF
CREATIVE MEDIA, INC.
P.O. Box 1
Minot, North Dakota 58702
701/852-5552

Printed in the United States of America

This book is dedicated to
the Stangland family,
within whose
sheltering influence
I grew up.

All characters in Onion Avenue are fictitious except the Stangland forebearers no longer living whose true stories in some cases are laced with fiction.

To suit the purposes of the novel the description of the actual Stangland farm has also been somewhat changed.

Author's grandmother
Elizabeth Stangland

Bela Stangland

Tallock Stangland

PROLOGUE

SCARLET PLUMAGE FLASHING against the snow-encrusted pine, a tufted redbird puffed his breast and whistled, AWAKE! AWAKE! His voice rose above the small woods that lay on the rise between the lake and the farmstead. Limbs of hickory, oak and maple snapped into place as their snowy burdens cascaded to the ground. Graying drifts sagged against fences. Under the dirt-edged mounds tiny rivulets tunneled their way to the lake where a rolling boom also announced the breakup of an icy winter.

But no human voice, no domestic intrusion broke into the harmony of bird, trees and lake. The Stangland farm, into its fourth generation, sat vacant. Two summers had passed with little to disturb the quiet ripples of the willow-shaded lake as bluegills and cropies swam its depths. In autumn there was no family to gather hickory nuts from the bursting pods.

The pasture lot was empty, the fields fallow, no visiting cousins joined a game of hide-and-seek in the big bank barn. No parents visited on the wide front porch; the old ice cream freezer sat in a corner rusting.

But the harbinger sensed a change. Cheer! Cheer! he called again.

Part One

CHAPTER 1

The Farm

KATHERINE ANDERSON DROPPED HER HOE and knelt to inspect the bushy green row of peas. Smiling, she rose and nodded. Now she could tell Ivan her peas were beginning to pod, matching his description of a pregnant cow "ready to calf."

Taking off her wide-brimmed garden hat that shaded an oval face with high cheek bones, she fanned a breeze into the waves of her chestnut-brown hair styled in a smart 1935 fashion. With pride, she looked around at the small thriving patch, a quarter of the big family garden Ivan's family had tended in past years. But with Kate's limited gardening ability it would have to do for this year.

Suddenly she looked at her watch, then hurried toward the house hoping she had not delayed too long. As she crossed the wide front porch to the screen door, she could hear the lid to the kettle of meat bobbling. Good, the fire had not gone out. With an iron hook she lifted the lid above the firebox and added a stick of wood. It responded with an obedient crackle. Into the stew pot she dumped the already prepared carrots, potatoes and onions and replaced the lid.

Starting back toward the garden, she paused beside the sturdy old porch swing and wanted to sink into it. But she was determined to finish hoeing the garden before dinner.

Kate was finally remembering to call the noon meal dinner like everyone else in this northern Indiana farm community. But getting it ready on time for Ivan when he came in for that brief hour, the only break in his long day of field work, was a problem.

Her new kerosene stove with the portable oven helped. It was similar to one her parents, who lived in Oregon, had up at their mountain cabin where there was no electricity either. But she must learn to use the wood range like other housewives in this community. On cold or chilly days it was needed for heat as well as cooking. At first she thought that stove cozy and quaint in the big old farm kitchen but that was before she had to depend on it for all the cooking. She flushed, remembering the times Ivan had come in for a meal and found her in tears because the fire went out and she had nothing ready to eat. He had been very patient, but finally bought her the kerosene stove. Kate knew he charged it and felt guilty.

A fidgety wren flew from her chalkbox house under the eaves to the nearby clothesline post. Peering down at her neighbor she scolded saucily.

Kate laughed. "No, Jenny, I didn't forget the fire today. I didn't forget to stoke that old monster and I'm going to have dinner ready on time." The wren flew about her business.

Before moving to the row of green beans, Kate leaned on the hoe, arched her back for relief and looked out across the fields glimmering with June: lush but lonesome. Cars went along the highway a quarter of a mile distant, otherwise there was not a person in sight.

The black-dirt fields were called "muck" by natives of the community. The term bothered her at first because she associated it with filth, but now she realized it was the fertile soil that produced big yellow onions, their bread and butter – and hopefully more. She had learned that long ago the whole area was one huge lake and the muck was silt left when the lake dried up. It was more lake than muck, Ivan told her, when in 1839 his Norwegian great grandfather, Andrew Stangland, came to this Indiana farm from New York state. Even now many old timers still referred to the area as Long Swamp, Ivan said.

Kate worried sometimes that she shouldn't have urged Ivan, with his college degree, to come back to the farm. He'd warned her that muck farming was a gamble; late or early frosts or too much rain could demolish a whole crop.

She wondered what her husband was doing and thinking at that very moment. Smiling, she pictured him in his shapeless farmer overalls with the galluses hooked over his shoulders, a straw hat covering his wheat-colored hair, curling at the ends from sweat. She often looked into his blue eyes and visioned a son with those eyes rather than her own which were light brown. Even though Ivan was only part Norwegian, he'd surely inherited the appearance and personality of a Norske.

Didn't he ever get tired she wondered? He began and ended each day with "chores" (caring for the farm animals and milking) after many hours in the fields. It meant daylight till almost dark every day except Sunday.

Kate, too, worked harder than she ever had in her life, or ever expected she would; but her labor did not compare to his. What had she accomplished in three months? It seemed so little beside what still had to be done. She had finally finished refurbishing the kitchen and bedroom, keeping the country mode she'd envisioned from the first.

Taking another moment's rest, she surveyed with dismay the overgrown, tangled mass of weeds and old dried grass along the house and corners of the steps. Trellises were tumbled over from the weight of untamed vines; flowers were struggling through thatch to reach the sun and bloom. Ivan lamented he didn't have more time to help her, but admitted he knew little about flowers or gardening. His mother and sister had always tended them.

Kate chided him, "That wasn't included in four years of studying agriculture?"

They both graduated a year earlier from the same Midwest college. Kate majored in art and interior design; Ivan in agriculture. As seniors they were mere acquaintances, but later in the suburbs of Chicago they found themselves working almost side by side. They began dating and fell in love.

One night at their favorite little Coney Island hot dog place, they lingered after finishing five coneys between them. After watching how well the Greek proprietors managed the place, Kate began asking Ivan about his Norwegian ancestry. He told her about the farm he was part heir to, now vacant and untended. She was instantly fascinated.

"It's been in your family for almost 100 years! Oh, Ivan, you mustn't sell it."

He was amused at her uncommon concern. "What are we going to do with it? My brother Claud doesn't want to farm. My sister Helga's husband has a farm already. We don't want to turn it over to some half-interested renter."

"Well, there's *you*, Ivan. Don't you know how to farm?"

Ivan leaned back in his chair and put his hands behind his head still watching her with love and amusement. "I'd be laughed out of the county. Four years of college to go back and farm?"

But Kate was serious. "What's wrong with an educated farmer?" Realizing how enthusiastic she had become, she flushed and added, "That is, if you want to do it."

After a long pause he leaned forward again and picked up her hands clasped on the table between them. "To tell you the truth I've been thinking a lot lately of doing just that."

"Oh, do it, Ivan. You must keep the farm in the family."

"I'm not sure I could make a very good living at it, at least not right away."

"But you'd be rich in so many other ways." Then barely loud enough to be heard over the din around them, she added, "The only thing is, I don't want you moving so far away from me."

Beneath the bright lights overhead, Ivan gazed at their intertwined fingers before he raised his eyes to meet hers. "Then how would you like to come with me and be a farmer's wife?"

"Oh, Ivan, I'd love it," she answered without hesitation. Many times since that night they had laughed at the "romantic" setting for his proposal.

The wedding had been at her family church in Portland. They'd traveled there by train, Kate a week ahead of Ivan. Both of their cars had been sold in Chicago so that they could buy a new 1935 Ford to drive back after the wedding. They brought along what wedding presents they could, many of them to store in the attic – appliances to be hooked to electricity they wouldn't have. And there would be no use for bath rugs and other such items in an outhouse.

Her parents had given them a sizable check, which Ivan insisted she keep, along with the other checks they'd received, in a separate account to spend on redecorating the house.

Traveling back to Indiana made a wonderful honeymoon. They drove short days, stopped at points of interest and looked for neat and clean tourist cabins for overnight. But as they progressed eastward, it was almost like going back in time from spring to winter. Spring had come early to the Northwest. Their wedding day had been beautiful, sunny and warm; all over town blossoms were emerging. But on their return trip they had encountered snow storms and high snow banks, especially in the mountain passes. However the two Andersons were blissfully happy in spite of the weather.

On the last day, as they approached their destination, Kate became more apprehensive. She was going to a house, a farm, a community she'd never seen before. Ivan kept telling her not to expect much; the farm needed a lot of work. How ramshackled would it be she kept wondering. She loved renewing things but how many possibilities would it have?

The day was dismal and chilly with misting rain. Ivan pointed out their nearest neighbors. From the tone of his voice, the neat white buildings of the Rockwells bore little resemblance to the old Stangland homestead. Ivan slowed to turn north off the highway where a mailbox on a slanting rotten post faintly proclaimed: ANDERSON RR#4. Kate clenched one hand beneath her purse, closed her eyes and breathed a final fervent prayer before she faced the home she could not now reject. I won't let him see one flicker of disappointment, she resolved. Then she slowly opened her eyes and looked past the bare maple trees which lined the rutted dirt lane.

The house was grayed with age but structurally handsome beneath the gently sloping roof broken by a wide dormer. Then her eyes focused on the low gray stone wall all along the front of the wide porch. For that brief interlude, while Ivan drove up and parked in front, she had gazed at the house unbelieving. This *was* the house of her dreams! Then with all the pent-up emotion of the long trip, Kate threw her arms around her husband, and shed tears against his cheek. "It's beautiful! It's perfect! Why didn't you ever tell me?"

She could feel Ivan's sigh of relief as he said huskily, "I didn't think it could mean much to you, the way it is now. I was so worried you should have seen it."

Kate smiled as she recalled the next incident. She stood on the front porch eager to enter. But after opening the door, Ivan stopped her, picked her up, carried her over the threshold and deposited her in the warm kitchen. The Rockwell neighbors had, on cue, left a fire burning. And even to Ivan's surprise, they had left a casserole of chicken and noodles in the oven and a warm cherry pie on the table. It was a precious memory she'd never forget.

During those next chilly long days with Ivan busy so much of the time, she often needed that warm memory to strengthen her resolve. She was struggling with an entirely new lifestyle in a strange house, in a new community and faced with constant frustrations. Even now after three months, she wondered if she was beginning to "get the hang of it" as her Dad would say.

Behind her she heard the rumble of Ivan's tractor coming toward the barn. She hurriedly gave a few last digs to complete the job, parked the hoe, then hurried toward the house. The dumplings to drop on top of the stew had to be made yet. She'd seen the recipe on the sack of pancake mix.

CHAPTER 2

Treasure In The Attic

THE TRACTOR'S STEADY DRONE and the jolt were pleasant to Ivan when things went well. Even though the ground was damp, the plow was cutting clean. Recent rainy weather had kept him out of this field. Now it was imperative that he get the last of the muck plowed, worked up and planted to onions.

Kate complained that he was working too hard. Well, not much harder than any other farmer during the season. He hated like the devil that they couldn't go out more often. But that would have to wait for fall and winter when a farmer is less busy.

The thought often troubled him that no matter how hard he worked he might not be able to provide Kate with many of the things she was used to. Shaky as the market is now, with the country just emerging from an economic depression, I can't predict anything, Ivan worried. Prospects for onions looked pretty good now, but who knows what they'll be by fall, even with a good crop.

As he alternately watched his steering and the plow following, he thought of the night he'd proposed to Kate at Coney Island Hot Dogs and she suggested he come back here. Had he been too hasty in agreeing to it? Her knowledge of farming came from story books, not reality.

Thinking of her, he smiled. He loved and appreciated the eagerness with which she tackled each new task, like the gardening. She was renewing and decorating the house with a vengeance, insisting that things should be kept a lot like they were. "Just a few modern touches," she'd told him. How he wished his parents could have known her.

With chagrin he thought of the old cookstove. That problem hadn't occurred to him. He just assumed all girls learned to cook as they grew up, like the farm girls he'd known. But even if she had learned, a wood range would be new to her.

His eyes rested on the large arrowhead tucked into a crevice of the fender. He'd found it that morning in the furrow when he opened the field. He picked it up and looked at it again: white stone chiseled down to a sharp point. How old was it? Who held the bow and what was he shooting at? Could his great grandfather Andrew have plowed it under 95 years ago when first he turned this virgin soil?

It occurred to Ivan that maybe that grandfather's problems might have been similar to his own – keeping a brave face while carrying doubts of whether he could support his family. He'd had a wife and five children when he came, with high expectations, to this farm. He had traded his 48-cultivated-acre farm near Kendall, New York, for 600 acres here in Indiana without having seen it.

It was a well-known story in the Stangland family, his mother's side, that a rich farmer from Numedal, Norway had bought a large farm in America, then had gone back to Norway and brought back 20 people to work for him to pay their passage. All but a few deserted or died from what was known as "swamp fever." Discouraged, the entrepreneur decided to sell and went back to New York looking for a buyer. He saw Andrew Stangland's farm, liked it, probably saw his chance to unload it on a trusting immigrant, and offered the whole 600 acres for Andrew's 48 with "two hundred dollars to boot." As the story goes, he set the bag of coins before his wife, Susan, when he came to supper late at his in-laws, the Carys.

Poor gullible great-grandfather Andrew, Ivan sighed, wondering if it ran in the family. When Andrew and Susan arrived in the spring of 1839 they found about one-third of the land under water and most of the rest too swampy to be farmable, which today, after years of ditching, was Ivan's valuable muck ground. But it took three generations to drain it. It was hard to say whether they had hung onto the farm for sentimental reasons or whether each Stangland down the line was too stubborn to admit he was beaten. Today the farm contained only 160 acres, but it was the best of the 600, with good fences and sturdy buildings, in need of paint though they were. A part of their present back porch was a remainder from the original home. Great-grandmother Susan must have settled into that house with delight after the long journey, just as Kate, the latest occupant, had thrilled to the present house.

Ivan approached the turn nearest the full-running ditch and flinched as it reminded him of another ditch. It had been three years now, since his parents drowned. The investigator for the accident said the Andersons had missed the bridge on county road 9 when they tried to cross it in the dark with water over the road. They weren't found for several hours so no one was sure just what happened. The court determined the county was at fault for not having markers out in time and it ended in a settlement which finished paying off the farm.

His brother Claud tried to run the place for the next couple of years with help from Ivan during his summers at home from college. But Claud was young and single, with little interest in farming as a career, especially with the bottomed-out market. Then they had tried to sell the farm and couldn't. So it sat vacant.

Ivan's was the first tractor ever on the Anderson farm and one of the few in the whole community. Earnie Rockwell, Rocky, had one, of course; he could afford it. Most of the men were still using horses. So badly hit by the depression, they were afraid to make changes. But to Ivan, putting a large share of his money into a tractor made sense. Fortunately he had found a bargain on one at a closing out auction. The same place he'd bought a herd of six cows and a small flock of laying hens.

There was too little high ground on his farm as it was without boarding horses; the pasture land and hay fields were needed for his cows. Some farmers thought the muck land was twice as valuable as the high ground. But that was in a good year.

Like his father, being a dairyman was Ivan's ambition. Maybe later he could find other land to rent or buy. He thought with envy about the original 600 acres.

Ivan looked at his watch. It was time to quit. He'd told Kate at noon he'd quit a little early, get his chores done and they would drive into town even if for no more than a tin roof sundae, her favorite. It was Saturday night and they should do something.

Before milking, Ivan went to the house to wash and get the milk pails. Kate, well-splattered with paint, came into the kitchen with a startled look on her face. "Is it that time already? I haven't even started supper."

He kissed her lightly on the lips and said, "Then I'll have an appetizer and finish the chores." He went to the screened-in porch where a wash basin sat on a bench with a pail of water beside it. He washed and threw the water out the back door, then went again to the kitchen, withdrew two slices of bread and piled it high with Serena Rockwell's applebutter. Kate had disappeared again. She was deep in some kind of decorating job, he was sure.

When he came in from milking, Kate had supper on the table – a dish she served often: left-over boiled potatoes fried with onion and scrambled eggs, always good.

"Do we still get to go into town for dessert?" she asked as they finished eating.

"That's why I quit early."

"I've got something to show you first." She took his hand and led him to the living room, then spread her arms dramatically. "Ta dah!"

She had painted around the bay window in an off-white. But it took a moment for Ivan to recognize the familiar piece she had placed there. It was the little old marble-topped table his mother had kept covered with a fringed cloth, discarded and stored when she got new furniture several years ago. It sat there now in gleaming glory, its oak foundation polished, the elegant white marble solid and clean beneath the teapot which sat on top.

"Where did you find it?" Ivan asked, amazed, visioning his mother's smiling approval.

Kate was bubbling over with the found treasure. "Up in the attic under the eaves when I was poking around. That's what kept me painting so long. I wanted to finish the bay window so I could show it to you in the right setting. I found the lovely old teapot way back in the top of the kitchen cupboard."

Ivan remembered it sitting at his mother's place almost every night. Too moved to speak, he put his arms around his wife and held her close.

CHAPTER 3

The Neighbors

KATE SAT IN THE OLD PORCH SWING hand-hemming chintz curtains to frame the bay window surrounding the marble-topped table. Glancing up she saw a dark-haired girl carrying a bowl emerge from the neat white Rockwell house at the head of the lane which joined the Anderson house to the highway. Michelle, usually called Shelly, slowly moved down the path, observing everything about her. To Kate she seemed so different from the rest of that hard working, practical family. The recent hard times had not affected the Rockwells as it had most farmers. Ivan described Earnie Rockwell as the kind of manager who could survive just about any adversity.

As Kate greeted Michelle she could see the blue-enameled bowl contained strawberries. Shelly held them out to her. "Mama said to tell you we wanted you to have a few berries even though there aren't many ripe yet."

"Thank you! What a treat we'll have for supper." Kate placed a welcoming hand on Michelle's arm. "Can you sit awhile?" The girl glanced back toward her house, then settled down on the stone wall that formed the front of the porch. Kate returned to the swing with the pan of berries in her lap, the chintz curtains beside her.

She had become fond of this girl of 14 and was always glad for her visits. She never stayed long nor talked much but Kate sensed a reaching out to her for something – understanding, perhaps. Her two older sisters and two young brothers were all big and blond like their father. Shelly had dark curly hair like her mother, Serena, but was average height and slim while her mother was large and robust, strong as a man. Michelle's eyes were like none other Kate had ever seen. One could hardly help from staring at them, not believing that eyes so big and blue and with such incredibly long, dark lashes could be real. However in those eyes Kate often detected a discontentment. But what girl of 14 was ever satisfied with her family or herself?

"Are you enjoying your vacation?" Kate began the conversation.

"I guess so," Shelly answered with little enthusiasm, "even though it's not much of a vacation. Just clean house . . . work in the garden . . . wash dishes. I hardly have any time to read or write or do the things I want to do."

What could Kate say to this restless girl and still remain loyal to her parents, their good neighbors? "I'll bet you'd like to take a vacation in town, wouldn't you? Like I always wanted to spend a summer in the country."

Shelly seemed surprised that Kate could guess her secret and sighed before responding. "I can only imagine what it would be like to go out of the house onto a city street, walk to the library or a store, or browse around a park with benches and a water fountain," she wrinkled her nose, "instead of a barnyard with a water tank for cows."

Kate laughed. "I understand how you feel. Once I dreamed about the country and here I am all grown up – and in it. The only trouble is I never realized the unpleasant aspects – no electricity and a wood stove to cook on. We pump every bit of water. And I used to think that would be fun!"

After a few moments Kate continued, "I had no idea how much work it is just raising chickens. I thought they ran around with their mothers like in the story books and grew up that way. I didn't know they were bought by the dozen and put under warmed metal hovers in brooder houses and need to be watched and fed so often." Kate laughed at herself. "And I never stopped to think that those gentle, grazing cows, such a picture in the field, have to be milked twice a day, every day, before and after the time city fellows go or come from work."

It suddenly occurred to Kate that she shouldn't be expressing her concerns to this already dissatisfied girl and changed the mood. "But on a beautiful June afternoon like this I feel like 'God's in His Heaven and all's right with the world.' "

"Robert Browning."

"I couldn't tell you who wrote it, but I picked up so many quotes from my big brother, Tommy. He loves poetry and read constantly when we were growing up. I suppose he still does. He chose books for a career."

Michelle's face brightened. "Oh . . . is he a writer?"

"He was always interested in writing but earns his living as a wholesale book distributor. He goes to book stores and other places to get their orders. Travels a lot, but he's single and thoroughly enjoys it."

"I didn't know there was a profession like that. But I suppose somebody has to distribute them . . . not a girl, though, I'm sure."

"Well, maybe someday, who knows? Women write books, why shouldn't they go on the road selling them?" Kate knew she had struck a note of interest in her young neighbor.

After a few more minutes, Shelly jumped up when she saw one of her sisters going from barn to house. "I was supposed to hurry right back."

"Tell your mother thanks so much for the strawberries. And do come down for a visit whenever you can, Michelle. We'll always have lots to talk about."

The girl smiled and hurried back up the lane. As Kate watched her, she remembered what Earnie Rockwell had said about her the first time Kate met the family. "Shelly was supposed to be a boy. I called her Mike before she was even born, but when it turned out she was a girl, her mother insisted on calling her Michelle – a name she got out of a book somewhere."

Carrying the pan of strawberries, Kate went to the kitchen to check the fire and the chili simmering over it, feeling that she had added a little leavening to the young girl's tedious day. Certainly Shelly was pleasant company, so mature for her age. Kate craved being able to talk to someone who understood her present lifestyle. Even though she kept up correspondence with girl friends, they wouldn't understand what she was going through. And Kate's interests and background seemed far removed from the farm women she had met so far.

During supper, they discussed the Rockwells over their dessert of strawberries. "They are about the givingest family around," Ivan said. "They give generously to the church. If anyone's in trouble they are the first to respond. He's with the volunteer fire department, the farm bureau . . . I don't know what all, and I doubt if anyone else does." Kate thought of her conversation with Shelly and how the girl needed something from her family that she wasn't getting, but didn't mention it to Ivan.

"Want to go with me back to the lake and see if the onions in that field are coming up yet?" Ivan asked when they finished eating.

"Oh, yes. Just wait till I change my shoes. I love going back there."

Little spikes of green were indeed starting to show. From the field they sauntered toward the little lake and spent nearly an hour taking a ride in the rowboat tethered there.

"Do you ever fish here?" Kate asked.

"No, I haven't for years. Other people do, but I've never been much interested. I guess it's a good thing; I wouldn't have time anyway."

When they got back to the house it was nearly dark. Ivan lighted the gasoline mantle lamp, a wedding present from the Rockwells, and they sat down to read the Fort Wayne Journal Gazette daily paper.

Just as they got settled, lights appeared coming down the lane. "Oh, dear, company's coming and I haven't even got the dishes washed," Kate said, wondering who it could be.

They heard car doors opening, quite a stir, then nothing as they waited for steps on the front porch. When there was still no knock, Ivan started to the door to investigate. Immediately bedlam broke loose. Horns honked, bells clanged, pails and tin cans rattled. The racket came from every direction.

Kate sat rigid with fright, unable to move, until she saw the look of amusement on Ivan's face as he quickly turned out the light. "I might have known!"

"Whatever is it?" All the weird happenings she'd ever heard of flitted through her mind.

"They're belling us." She could hear him quietly moving around in the dark.

"What?!!"

"Sh-h-h. Belling – shivaree." He handed her a coat. Yes, she'd heard of shivaris, but always connected them with foreign countries, or with times long ago. She hadn't the least idea what was expected of her or what would happen to them.

"We're supposed to try to escape. Let's try the back door. If we make it, run for the car," he whispered. Groping around in the dark, he found her shaking and hugged her. "It's nothing to be afraid of, honey. Just a bunch of noisy fun."

They had barely got through the back door when several pairs of hands grabbed them. There was a mighty shout, "Here they are! We've got them!"

They were pulled from each other. There must have been half-a-dozen boys manhandling Ivan as he shouted, "Hey, we've been here three months. We're old timers."

"That's OK. You haven't treated us yet," Kate heard someone shout back.

A young boy and girl, probably of high school age, were pulling Kate along to wherever they were taking Ivan. Somehow she expected the whole crowd to be wearing masks or hoods but, by the headlights of the several cars, she could see they were all just laughing, noisy young people, not in the least disguised.

As Kate passed the cab of a big truck she saw the printing on its door:

CARL FULLENBERG
STOCKHAULING
ONION CENTER

They pushed Ivan up the stock chute ahead of her, then she found herself dumped in beside him and they sat there laughing together on a small pile of straw. There was the strong smell of livestock. Kate cautiously looked around to be sure they were not sharing this vehicle with a pig, a sheep, or a cow. But there was only the straw and the high sturdy rack.

A couple of boys put up the chute, slammed in the end gate, then ran around and climbed in with the driver. The truck roared to a start. The banging and clanging ceased and the honking intensified as a stream of cars followed the truck down the lane.

"For heavens sake, where are they taking us?"

Ivan was still laughing, she wasn't sure whether with her or at her. "They'll take us over all the rough roads in the township, then back home again. That's all."

"That's all!"

And a rough and rugged half hour it was. The stock rack constantly jiggled and clattered as they bounced and joustled around on the floor of the truck. Mud splashed in on them as the truck ground into soft ruts. The horns continued to honk intermittently. It was also chilly. Kate appreciated the big, wool-plaid mackinaw Ivan had found for her.

Finally the whole party stopped around the truck in the little village of Onion Center – a couple of grocery stores, a garage and a gas station.

"Treats! Treats!" The crowd shouted from their car windows. "You got to treat us, Ive, for the ride."

"Let me out of here then," Ivan said as he stood up and the end gate promptly dropped. Both grocery stores were closed, so he entered the filling station.

"How did you like your ride, Mrs. Anderson?" a young voice called.

"It will do me till our fiftieth anniversary." How many of these people would she eventually come to know. She noticed the older Rockwell girls in the group, but apparently Shelly hadn't been allowed to come.

Ivan came out with an assortment of candy bars heaped in a box, and started passing them around.

"Thank YOU, Ive," Kate heard someone say.

"Ye'ah, after you twist both arms and knock my backbone out of place." There was more laughter.

The crowd began breaking up. Cars were leaving, couples sitting very close together. There were only two vehicles left to escort the truck and the now-initiated Andersons back to the farm. They were helped out more gently this time. Hand in hand they ran to their front door by the beam of the head-lights. There was a final honk, a "Goodnight, you lucky Andersons," and the cars and trucks departed up the lane.

Ivan took a match from his pocket and lighted the kerosene lamp on the kitchen table. Kate slipped off the big coat and took her choice, a Babe Ruth, from the few candy bars left in the box, sat down by the table and began eating it.

She laughed. "I feel like a clock that's sprung. What an ordeal. I had no idea such goings-on still took place." She went around and sat on his lap, put a hand under his chin and frowned. "How many of these shindigs have *you* been on that there was such a big turn out for us?"

"Now you know I've always been just a quiet country boy!"

"Um-hum," she murmured, hugging him hard.

CHAPTER 4

A Feud?

THE FOLLOWING MONDAY NOON when Ivan and Kate were finishing dinner, he asked, "Would you mind going into Richland for some little chicken mash this afternoon? They'll have to have feed before tomorrow."

"Sure, I'll go. I'd enjoy it. But aren't you afraid I'll get lost so far away from home alone?" she teased.

"Just send up a smoke signal." He gave her the necessary information and some money, kissed her goodbye and left for the field.

Kate hurriedly washed the dishes. She had finally arrived at her own system for doing them. She washed them in a pan on the drainboard of the corner sink, which had no faucets, and stacked them in a rack over the drain. To rinse them she poured on hot water from the old teakettle always simmering on the stove. The Rockwells did their dishes in two big pans on the cookstove, washing in one, draining in the other, then drying them with a towel. Perhaps that was because they had more dishes to do and more people to use the sink. Kate had trouble getting used to hand washing, shaving and pan baths, then dishwashing at the same sink. She scrubbed it often.

As Kate dressed for town she was surprised at herself for being so excited about going by herself into a little country town for chicken feed! How dried up I've become in three months, she thought. Did other brides feel this loss of freedom?

She noticed the money Ivan had laid out for her. It was from the bi-weekly milk check, their only current source of income. And so much of it was spent to feed the animals.

Arriving in Richland, she stopped first at the feed mill where local grain – corn, wheat or oats – was ground into different size particles to match the needs of growing livestock or poultry. The workers eyed her curiously. So this was the new wife of Ivan Anderson, a boy they'd grown up with. She was sure some of them had been at the shivaree.

From the mill she drove on into the center of town and parked by the courthouse square where several other cars were already parked. There was even a horse and buggy, apparently from the Amish community. Since Richland was the county seat, considerable business took place there, along with grocery shopping and the buying of minor merchandise. For major shopping trips most people drove into Fort Wayne.

Across from the courthouse was the Kroger store where Kate and Ivan sold their eggs and bought most of their groceries. Next to Krogers was Merlin's drugstore and next to that was the popular Sweet Shop. They had the best and biggest sundaes and ice cream cones anywhere around, or so Ivan insisted. Now after several visits Kate agreed. She'd pass it up today, though, with no one to share a treat with.

Kate bought the few groceries she needed, then went to the variety store to buy some curtain hooks. Still not wanting to go home, she browsed through cosmetics and lingerie. Finally from the rack of candy, she chose two Clark bars to enjoy with Ivan after supper.

She took the long way home, still reluctant to get back too soon. It was over a road she had been on only once and with Ivan. As she approached the highway, a quarter of a mile or so from their lane, she was attracted to a derelict little farm. The house, the small barn and the other out buildings gave the appearance of general neglect. But in spite of the unkemptness of the buildings, there was an abundance of well-tended flowers, dashes of color here and there in a profusion of spring.

She slowed to get a better view when a woman in an old-fashioned calico sunbonnet rose with difficulty from the little garden at the side of the house. It must be one of their neighbors she hadn't met or even heard of, Kate decided. She pulled up in front of the house, stopped the car and approached the garden fence, pausing long enough to smell the climbing roses over an arbor.

"Isn't it a lovely day?" Kate addressed the woman with friendly assurance. The woman did not answer but eyed Kate suspiciously and did not move from the spot where she stood. She probably thinks I'm selling something. Or maybe she's hard of hearing, Kate decided. "I'm Katherine Anderson, Mrs. Ivan Anderson." Then, a little louder, "I was going by and . . ."

"I can hear you, girly. I ain't deef even if I am old." Beneath the sunbonnet, the woman's face was deeply lined, her shoulders were thin and stooped. "Yer man one o' Arthur Anderson's boys? You live down there on thet place?" The woman indicated the general direction of their farm with a jerk of her head.

Kate's self-confidence withered. "Yes-s, my husband is the younger brother; we just took over the farm three months ago." Had Ivan's brother Claud caused some bitterness here, Kate wondered.

"If yer any part o' that tribe o' Andersons, you ain't got no business here. Git along with ya' now!" The old woman shouted in a crackling angry voice, waving one arm as though she could will away her unwelcome visitor with one sweep of her bony hand.

Kate felt completely crushed. Her first impulse was to say nothing more, just hurry away to the privacy of her car. But this was a neighbor, perhaps for years to come. Whether this woman lived here alone, with a son or a daughter . . . she had no way of knowing. She realized now she shouldn't have stopped on impulse only. But now that she was here, she must make an effort to smooth over the incident, even if the woman were out of her mind. She looked hopefully toward the house for someone else to appear.

"I'm very, very sorry," Kate faltered, gripping the fence to stop herself from shaking. "I had no idea Andersons weren't welcome here. Everyone has been so wonderfully kind since I came. Your flowers looked so pretty as I was passing by . . . I just couldn't help but stop and meet another neighbor."

"Ain't you been told Mattie Enders an' Andersons don't neighbor fer over fifteen years now?" The voice was lower now with less edge.

Kate flushed deeply at the thought of a possible feud she hadn't been told about. "Why no! Ivan is such a friendly fellow; I had no idea he had any enemies."

"Well, if yer man's eny good he ain't much like his father. Couldn't trust him a'tall." Mattie Enders took a few steps forward and dropped one hand from the hoe, leaving Kate feeling a little less threatened. "Ain't seen much o' the boys, nor the girl neither since they was little."

"I'm so sorry to hear about this," Kate said. "I didn't know Ivan's father. In fact, I haven't met any of the rest of his family yet. I hadn't even seen the farm until after we were married. I'm sure I would have liked his mother. I love the house and so many of her things I'm finding there." Kate took a long shaking breath and gathered courage to go on. "Actually your flowers were the biggest reason I stopped. So many of them look to be the same as what is coming on down there, only, of course, not so well taken care of. I know so little about flowers; my mother took care of them at home. I don't know what they are or what to do with them. I thought maybe you might come down and give me some advice."

The prospect of visiting the Anderson place obviously gave Mattie Enders a jolt. She raised her hand and opened her mouth as though to start shouting again, then seemed to change her mind as she faced this already frightened girl. She avoided Kate's eyes. "Well, I might come down sometime jest long enough to name yer posies fer you. Wouldn't go in the house, of course. If I could count on a time when there ain't none o' them Andersons 'round. It's likely most o' them flowers down there is the same as mine. Nan an' me used to exchange starts an' bulbs."

"I'd appreciate that so much. I'll drive up after you someday when I'm sure Ivan is going to be gone all afternoon."

"Don't need to come a-drivin' up here after me. I ain't feeble, I can walk across the fields. Just ring a long an' a short on yer phone."

"I'll surely do that some day soon." Relieved, Kate turned back towards the car after a cheery, "Goodbye and thanks a lot."

Mattie Enders said nothing, just bent down beneath her faded bonnet and returned to digging vigorously with the hoe.

That evening over supper, Ivan asked about her trip to town. Kate told him every detail up to the strange encounter with the old woman. "I came back over the Johnson road. It must have been scraped down because it's pretty smooth, hardly a rut in it."

"Good." Ivan went on eating without further reaction.

"Who lives in that neglected little place just as you turn onto the highway from that road?"

She saw his color rise but he asked calmly, "Which side of the road? You mean west from Martins?"

"Yes, almost across from Rockwells." He knew perfectly well where she meant. He was hedging, but why? And she was just as unwilling to tell what a blunder she'd made.

"Oh, that's old lady Enders' place. Mattie Enders. She's pretty old, getting senile too, I imagine. Doesn't get around much."

"Does she live there alone?"

"As far as I know she does. She had a son, Robert, but he died several years ago."

"No wonder everything looks so neglected – except the flowers, they're beautiful. Who farms for her, Mr. Rockwell?"

"No, some young kid, I don't remember his name. Just graduated from high school. I talked to him a few minutes over the fence when he was plowing."

"Oh, some of her property joins ours? Would it be a good chance for you to get more ground, maybe next year?"

Ivan's jaw settled into an almost angry look. "Seems like I've got as much as I can handle here for now."

"Well, she's sure got some lovely flowers anyway." She'd let it go at that.

As Ivan went back out to finish his chores, he worried about the conversation. Sooner or later he'd have to tell Kate about Mattie Enders' bitterness toward his family for so many years. She might stop to visit the old lady or something. Kate would think it ridiculous. He thought so too, but it seemed there was no changing Mattie Enders.

Maybe he should try to find some way to neighbor again, but old Mattie's bitterness had probably simmered so long it was ingrained in her. He had thought maybe at the time his parents died she might come around of her own accord, but never a word or a card. Claud and Helga didn't seem to care. They mostly laughed about it. But in Ivan the hurt was still there. Perhaps because it was he who used to visit her son, Robert, more often than they did. He was never told what happened to Robert or why it turned Mattie into a recluse and embittered her against their family.

CHAPTER 5

Sad Story

ON A RAINY JUNE DAY Ivan couldn't get into the fields and after chores he suggested they make one of their infrequent trips into Fort Wayne. He wanted to compare the price of a tractor-pulled cultivator against the price the dealer in Richmond had quoted. "We won't have much money to spend, but we can surely spare enough to go to Coney Island for some hot dogs."

Kate was delighted and hurried through a minimum of her morning work.

As they began their trip, rain beating against the windshield, Kate said, "While we are driving in, why don't you tell me the story of your great grandparents. You never have, you know."

"All right. But like I told you, it's not a happy story."

★ ★ ★ ★

In the spring of 1839 Andrew Stangland moved from New York state to Indiana with his wife, Susan, and their five children: Eleazer 10; Tallock 7; Bela 6; Rosetta 3; and Maria 2 months. Left behind in her little grave on their former farm was the second born child, Lydia, who died at 3 months, nine years earlier.

Sadly Andrew's expectations of being the land owner of a very large western farm withered when he arrived at the site where clouds of mosquitoes hovered over the swampy ground.

Nevertheless, the house was a delight to Susan. It was not as attractive as the little house Andrew had built for her in New York as a bride; but the long dormitory-like building adjoining the main house would give them all the room they could possibly need. It had been built to house the 20 workers the former owner had brought from Norway to work for him and pay their passage over. Bunks were curtained off into little compartments on either side. Never again would three brothers have to sleep in the same bed. And Susan could envision clotheslines along the length of the room for use in bad weather. There were enough fireplaces to warm both the main house and the extra building.

Several pieces of furniture had been left behind by the Orslands and Susan set about making her new home comfortable.

Andrew's farming problems were not so easily solved. All he could do the first year was farm the high ground patches. On one of them the house and small pole barn sat. He could see where the former owner had had his workers digging a ditch by hand in an attempt to drain some of the land into the lake. But it hadn't helped much; the low ground was still unfarmable.

A plow had been left on the place and Andrew had brought two horses, Cloud and Misty, who pulled the wagon they moved in. So he began plowing the high ground the day after they arrived. And from then on for the next several years, nearly every hour he could spare from his crops or farm chores he worked at draining swamp land. After harvesting the first crop from the black silt-like soil he realized how valuable it was. Corn seemed to spring up overnight and produced heavier than he'd ever known. But getting the soil drained was an exhausting life. Nevertheless he kept at it without admitting he'd been duped. A Norwegian who'd come seeking land in America and had fallen owner to 600 acres would not be stopped by hard work. He toiled on the land with the help of his young sons. While Susan, with the help of sturdy little Rosetta, toiled over a big garden, canning, cooking, sewing, mending, bearing more children and encouraging all of them with their education.

Eleazer became interested in honey bees and tended several round hives of them. Tallock and Bela tapped the few sugar maple trees found in the woods by the lake. Andrew and Susan helped found a Christian church in the community as well as a cemetery. Susan and her close neighbor, Sara Ott, often went with their young children to welcome newcomers to the area, taking along a pie, cookies or fresh baked bread. Life was not easy for the Stanglands but they prospered as much as most of the farmers in the community in the Midwest of the 1840s.

Nearly every summer Susan's parents, the Carys, came to visit and continued on up to Michigan for a visit with their son, James, Susan's older brother. Sometimes one or more of the small children would go back with the grandparents to spend some time. Then one of the twin uncles, Alexander or Leander, or Mr. Cary himself would bring them back and do some hunting or fishing where game was plentiful. Almost the entire trip could now be made by canal boat and rail car.

To complete their family of eight, the three children born to Susan and Andrew after moving to Indiana were: Andrew Jackson (Jack), Mary Elizabeth (Libby) and Benjamin Franklin (Frank).

Eight years of unrelenting labor with too little rest was taking its toll on Andrew. After the heavy wheat harvest of 1847 he contacted pneumonia and didn't recover. On August 31, one day before his 49th birthday, Andrew Stangland died, leaving behind in unconsoleable sorrow his wife of 20 years and eight children – one of them still in the womb.

Little Frank was born 5 months after his father's death. But Susan's spirit was broken; she was never the same. For the most part the older boys, Eleazer 18 and Tallock 15, took over. Susan cooked, mended and cleaned silently and mechanically, letting the children take care of each other.

In bearing her ninth child, Susan had spent six of the twenty years she'd been married (at 16) in a state of pregnancy, so she accepted it as a normal condition. But sometimes when she was by herself she would alternately cry and sing to the child within her. It was the last living thing her beloved Andrew had left her.

After the birth of little Frank in January 1848, Susan lived until the following November 4. She was bedfast through October and near the end of the month she asked for the four older children to come to her bedside after they had put the little ones to bed.

For a little while she gazed into four sober faces, then finally she spoke. "I think before long now, I'll be going to join your father."

"Oh, no, no, Mama," eleven-year-old Rosetta cried, falling by the side of the bed.

"Be brave, Rosetta," the mother said as she reached a weak hand out to her. "You're already a good housekeeper and God will give all that you need." She looked up at her three stalwart sons, tears flowing down their faces. "Grandma and Grandpa will come and take you all back to New York where you can help on their farm or someone else's." Susan, gasping for breath, had to rest; her eyes closed against tears she was trying to suppress. She wanted to think only of reuniting with Andrew in a place of peace. They had raised good children and she had confidence in them.

She was finally able to continue. "Mrs. Young will nurse and take care of little Frankie, like she has been, until he, too, is ready to go to Grandma Cary or Aunt Martha and Uncle James."

Eleazer, always the comforter, leaned his tall, lanky frame over the bed and kissed her cheek, "We'll take care of them, Mama, so they won't be a burden on Grandma and Grandpa."

Susan reached up and clung to his hand, "I know you will, Leazer, you always have."

A few days later, with the doctor and the older children by her side, Susan breathed her last.

Eleazer immediately took over the family with the help of many willing neighbors. But what Susan hadn't realized in her weakened and distraught condition was that the grandparents, although notified, could not get through during the winter to the Indiana farm. So the eight orphaned children took care of themselves under Eleazer's leadership. He delegated duties to every child old enough to do anything at all. Tallock was to head up the farm operation, which in winter consisted mainly of caring for the livestock.

With the approach of spring, there was controversy between the two older brothers. Tallock wanted to put out crops and remain on the farm, but Leazer forbade it, saying that he could not stay there alone and he was going back to New York and continue his dream of training to be a doctor. With the grandparents on Leazer's side there was little Tallock could do but go along back to New York.

So in the spring of 1849, just ten years after Andrew and Susan's arrival, the farm was vacated for the first of three times in its nearly 100 years as a Stangland farm.

★ ★ ★ ★

By the time Ivan finished the story, and the rain continued around them, tears were also running down Kate's cheeks. She wiped them away with her fingertips and laid her head on Ivan's shoulder. He held her hand tightly. "But you got to remember old Grandpa Tallock was a stubborn Norwegian, too. He didn't give up his dream either."

CHAPTER 6

A Challenge

MICHELLE ROCKWELL RELAXED into the mow of fresh cut alfalfa hay, which had been hauled in and lifted in a sling to the barn loft just the day before. Her brothers, Joe 10, Jimmy 8 and her sister Mary 17 had helped while she and her other sister, Clara 18, had to help their mother finish up the meat from the butchering: rendering out the lard and frying down sausage to chill in lard and use later. And stuffing sausage – in slimy old pig guts. She grimaced. Clean as her mother got those casings, they were still pig guts!

She opened a poetry book which had been tucked under her apron when she sneaked off to the barn. Actually, she was supposed to be hoeing in the garden, or so Clara said when she found her in the hammock reading. But since it was Clara who told her instead of her mother or dad, Michelle didn't feel very guilty.

It was nice up there now, but later the loft would be too full of hay and too hot so close to the roof. Then she'd escape to the thicket by the Anderson woods near the lake. If she sat very quiet, she could see a variety of birds – a cardinal flashing by, a red-winged blackbird or a gorgeous little bluebird, her favorite. Once one lighted on a branch only a few yards away and sang its heavenly melody. Enchanting little creatures, so beautiful – and so free.

She turned her head now, ever so carefully, so not to frighten away the nesting pair of barn swallows carrying mud in their bills to build a home up under the eaves. They were blue, but not so blue as bluebirds. Their long slender bodies were followed by deeply split tails, and they flew differently from other birds she knew. A flutter of wings and a zip, then another flutter of wings and a zip, almost like skiing she imagined. It must be nice to live in a place where you could learn to ski in winter or go canoeing down the river in the summer. Here there was nothing but lakes.

She heard Jimmy calling, "Shelly! Shelly!" What did the little pest want now? Well, she didn't have to answer to him either. After several more calls his voice died away.

A little later she heard Clara and Mary talking as they came from out of the house. They came within hearing range and she heard Clara say, "She can think of more ways to get out of work."

Mary said, "She must think she's a queen bee or something."

Then Michelle heard Joe asking eagerly, "After we get the chicken feed can we go to the Sweet Shop?" She sat upright, ready to bolt down the ladder and call to them. But her pride held her back. The car doors slammed and the motor started.

Tears streamed down Michelle's cheeks. It wasn't just the missed opportunity to go into town but the hurt of hearing what her sisters thought of her. Why, why, why was she dropped into this family who thought of nothing but working and eating. She cried bitter tears into the new mown hay.

★ ★ ★ ★

Kate had been washing all morning on the back porch on the old Thor washing machine. The gasoline motor continued its loud putt-putt-putt through each load in the same water. First the white things, then the colored load and finally Ivan's muck-covered overalls, which left the water looking like black ink. The system was similar to what Kate was used to, except for the gasoline motor. "It's a noisy way to wash, but beats going back to the lake and pounding it out with a rock," she laughingly commented as Ivan helped her carry out the dirty water and empty it behind the wood shed.

At dinner Ivan said, "I have to go into Richland this afternoon to get a piece welded on that cultivator. Do you want to go along?" He had been fortunate to find a used cultivator in Fort Wayne, one he could afford without charging.

"How long will you be?"

"Between getting that done and the other things I have to do, it might be most of the afternoon."

Kate hesitated. What would she do in Richland all afternoon? "No, I think not, if you'll get me some more paint. I'm going to start on that little downstairs bedroom next."

"Do you want pink or blue?" he asked mischievously.

She stuck out the tip of her tongue at him. "Neither one, nosy, I want green, light green and I've got a color chip to send along."

After Ivan left she stood looking after him. Then her eyes wandered over toward the little farm of the old lady, Mattie Enders. An idea popped into her head. It was such a nice day, did she dare? Ivan would be gone for several hours.

She went to the telephone and lifted the receiver cautiously, then hung it up and stood wondering. Was she summoning danger, asking the old lady over without really knowing much about her? Maybe she should ask Mrs. Rockwell first. Ivan had said the woman was senile if not worse. What did he know about her? She rang the phone quickly before she had any more time to talk herself out of it. After a brief interval, during which Kate almost hoped no one would answer, she heard the click of the other receiver being lifted.

"Hullo!" the coarse voice said loudly.

"Hello, this is Kate Anderson. Ivan is away for the afternoon, I was wondering if you could come down for a little while to go over the flowers with me?"

There was a long pause. "T'day's as good as eny day, I guess."

"Are you sure you don't mind walking down?"

"Why should I? I've walked it many a time. I'll be along as soon as I git my bonnet an' my sleeves on."

Kate heard the receiver click, then she also slowly hung up, wondering if anyone else on the party line had heard the brief conversation. She supposed the whole community knew about this silly feud.

She sat down trying to invent tactful ways to ask the questions she wanted answered. Finally she gave up. After all, she wasn't being honest, scheming to get something out of this strange old woman whether she wanted to tell it or not. She had asked her down to look at the flowers, nothing more.

Kate watched Mattie Enders push open the last gate which separated the fields from the Anderson's front yard, squeeze through, and lift it shut again. She went out on the front porch to meet her. "I don't know how you made those fences. I haven't tried them yet, but I don't think I could."

Mattie reached the stone steps and dropped on them, taking off her sunbonnet and fanning herself with it, saying nothing, just breathing heavily. Kate sat down in the swing. With the bonnet off she could really see Mattie

Enders for the first time. Her face was blanched and drawn, probably because she always wore the bonnet. What there was of her hair was iron gray and barely covered her head. The ends were pinned into a small, tight knot at the top of her head. The dark blue high-necked calico smock – her "sleeves" she'd said – was neat and clean.

"Beginnin' to think thet field's wider than it used to be. 'Course it's been a spell since I crossed it." Mattie's breathing was beginning to slow down, but she sat in silence another minute or so. Kate waited patiently, then nervously in need of doing something, moved down and pulled some weeds growing at the side of the steps.

"Nan used to have a clump o' Star O' Bethlehem there at the corner o' the steps. Eny of it left now?"

"Here? I haven't seen anything that looks like flowers in this corner."

"I suppose that man Arthur pulled 'em up or mowed 'em off. What's thet over there by the fence? Looks like 'em." Mattie replaced her bonnet, got up slowly, went to the side fence and pushed down the grass almost hiding the dainty flowers. "Yes, sure that's them. An' here's the Blue Bells."

"The name certainly fits the flowers."

"I bet she was tryin' to git the red, white an' blue together like I've got. Don't see eny Bleedin' Heart." The strange old woman poked about in the grass. Kate waited and wondered what she was talking about.

"I always keep my Blue Bells, Star O' Bethlehem an' Bleedin' Heart together, one behind the other so it's red, white an' blue fer Decoration Day. They all bloom 'bout thet time."

"Oh, yes, I know now. Bleeding Heart is a red, heart-shaped flower on a tall stem. No, I haven't seen any of that around." Kate smiled to herself. This old neighbor knew perfectly well what she was saying and doing. "I'd like that arrangement. Only I think I'll move it back by the steps if I can get some Bleeding Heart."

"Stop in someday when you're goin' by. I'll give ya' a clump fer each side o' the steps. I got it fixed up thet way on Robert's grave. He was my son. Does look real purty."

Almost an hour passed as the two went from place to place about the yard and the garden: "Was there anythin' left o' Nan's purple Clematis vine? Yes, here it is, fallen to the ground. Needs tyin' up again . . . this is a yella' rose here by the orchard fence . . . There's the white an' purple flags by the back fence. Her lilacs bloom late. Guess mine must be a li'l more pertected. Wonder if you could let me have a shoot from thet white lilac bush someday. Mine winter-killed year 'fore last."

Kate followed her around, answering and remarking briefly but with lively interest, learning much and getting ideas. Mattie remembered every detail of the place after so many years. How many, Kate wondered. They must have been very close neighbors. What a pity the friendship ended.

Kate looked at her watch. Three o'clock. Mrs. Enders seemed to be in no hurry to leave, there was still time before Ivan was due back. "Would you have a cup of tea with me?" she asked timidly. When Mrs. Enders didn't answer, looking almost as though she hadn't heard, Kate supposed she'd blundered again and continued with what came to her mind first. "I never know if I dare ask that in this community. People never seem to stop in the middle of the afternoon for coffee like we so often do back home. They seem only to take time out for meals here."

"I live alone so I don't have to ask nobody when I can or can't drink tea."

"Good. Then I'll make us some even though I haven't a thing to go with it."

She had just got the hot water poured over the tea in the pink-roses teapot, thinking the old neighbor might recognize it, when she heard her exclaim: "That looks like yer man comin' now! I'll be gittin' back across the field. Have to have my tea ta home."

Kate hurriedly sat the teapot down and went to the door. It wasn't even Ivan, just someone going past on the way to the lake or woods. But Mattie was already through the gate and hurrying across the field without a goodbye or a turn of the head. If it were anyone else, Kate would have felt highly insulted, but she'd had enough success already for one afternoon.

So she had a son buried in the graveyard, Kate reflected. She spoke of him as though he were still around. Had he died as a child? Was he a soldier? Was her husband buried there, too?

The telephone rang, two shorts and two longs. It was Serena Rockwell. "Are you all right?" her neighbor asked after a slight hesitation.

"Yes, yes, I'm fine." Kate wondered at the slight concern in Mrs. Rockwell's voice. "Is there something the matter?" She stepped to look out the window by her side. Maybe Mattie Enders had fallen or something.

"Forgive me but I couldn't help but see who your company was hurrying home just now. I just . . . wondered."

Kate laughed. "Actually I'd invited her down without Ivan knowing about it to give me some advice on my flowers. She got frightened away because she thought that car that came down the lane was him."

"Well, I never! We might have known it would take someone like you to bring her across." Neither of them wanted to say more about it on the phone. "I see my children coming home now," Serena continued. "They all went into Richland after chicken feed, all but Shelly. She was feeling kind of blue because she got left behind so I told her she could read."

"Thanks for calling, Serena, it's nice to be looked out for."

She didn't tell her neighbor that Ivan had never told her about the breech between the Andersons and Mattie. And I won't tell Ivan yet that she was here today, Kate decided. It wasn't likely the Rockwells would mention it to him. There seemed to be something very hush-hush about it. To do something in this community no one else can do. That would be nice. Very nice indeed.

CHAPTER 7

Sunday Dinner

KATE CHIPPED A CUP in her haste to finish the breakfast dishes, at the same time keeping watch over the big pot roast browning in the sizzling fat over the kerosene burner. There was the last minute picking up to do yet, besides making the bed and getting herself ready. The fruit salad had to be finished – oh, the cream! She must get it before the milkman came. She picked up a bowl, stopped to turn the meat once more, took the long-handled dipper from the drawer and went on the run to the porch. With some difficulty she jerked off the lid from the ten-gallon milk can sitting in a tub of cold water. It was nearly full of last night's milk with the rich cream thick at the top. Kate dipped up a generous amount into the bowl. Just as she was replacing the lid, Ivan came to the door with the last of the morning's milk to add to the other large can.

"Uh-huh, caught you again."

"Oh, don't scold me this morning, I'm too busy. With all those cows I still don't see why we shouldn't have all the cream we want."

"Take what you want, I was only joking." He set down the pails of milk. "Sunday's the best time anyway. They don't very often take a butter-fat test on Sunday. Some farmers even cheat by pouring in a pail of water."

Kate silently took the bowl of cream back to the kitchen feeling more than a little guilty. What was that old story about the cobbler's children going without shoes? Now the farmer's wife can't use cream.

She had been so keyed up all week over this impending visit from Ivan's sister and family, she began to wonder why she had suggested they invite them to a Sunday dinner. Would Helga approve of what she'd done to the house? What would she think of such a small garden? Would her lack of culinary skills be obvious? Would she even approve of Kate, herself, as a wife for her brother?

Ivan poured the last of the milk through the big metal strainer lined with gauze, waited for it to drain, then brought pails and strainer in to be washed.

"For heavens sake, honey, slow down, you'll be a nervous wreck. Helga and Harry aren't people to worry about. They're just plain farmers like around here."

"The difference is Helga grew up in this house. She'll notice everything whether she mentions it or not. Now go away and don't start giving me sympathy or I'll probably break into tears and I don't have time for that. If you want to make yourself useful, wash the milk pails and put them away." She moved back to the roast, poured a little water onto it and quickly replaced the heavy aluminum cover, turned out the stove, lifted the cover on the burner and carried the kettle across to the range. Helga wasn't going to catch her depending on a kerosene stove.

Without further words Ivan washed the milk pails and strainer, scalded them well, then turned them up in the sun of the back porch to dry. He stood around momentarily wondering whether he should ask if there was anything else he could do for her. She ignored him, so he decided against it and went on out to turn the cows into the pasture and finish the chores.

Half an hour later, through the bedroom window, Kate saw Ivan with his foot on the fender of the milk truck, casually laughing and talking to the milkman. It irritated her to see him so nonchalant when she was so flustered and busy. But after all it was Sunday, a day to relax. She was the one acting like a maniac. She sat down on the bed and made herself relax. Helga would have to take things as they are. It was too late to change anything now – even if she should. It was their house and their life. She got up and began dressing slowly and carefully, trying to calm herself.

When Ivan returned to the house, he found his wife prettily dressed, aproned and smiling. "Is it safe to touch you now?"

She kissed him as an apology. "No, you have to wash the cow smell off and get ready."

Two hours later, the Clodfelter family – Helga, Harry and their two children, Raymond and Shirley – joined Kate and Ivan around the dining room table.

To Kate the food seemed tasteless. The meat was dry, the vegetables over cooked, the fruit salad seemed too thin, the gravy too thick. She sat with her back to the marble table since she was using it for extra serving dishes, and ate as little as she could get by with. She was trying to believe what her mother had so often said: "A meal always tastes better to the company than to the cook." Helga's chicken and noodles were delicious. She noticed her family ate more of them than anything else. They had brought along a pie too, luscious-looking cherry, so Ivan wouldn't need to go after the ice cream to go with the cookies she'd baked on Saturday. They could have it later in the afternoon.

"What's this stuff?" four-year-old Raymond asked his mother, nudging the salad plate next to him.

"That's salad." The mother glanced across at Kate's reaction. Kate turned her attention to Harry who was talking and pretended not to hear.

"Salad! I'm not going to eat it."

"Hush," said his mother.

Kate winked at the boy and smiled. "You don't have to eat it if you don't want to. But it's got whipped cream in it. You better try it."

"I don't like salads," he persisted.

"Raymond! Eat your dinner and keep still." This was from the father, a tall, dark, serious-looking man who had little to say compared to his talkative wife.

Kate laughed, still unruffled. "Your Aunt Kate will have to remember next time that you don't like salads. But you know I come from the West where we eat lots of salad, all kinds."

"Out West where the cowboys are?" six-year-old Shirley said and gazed at Kate enchanted.

"Well, I don't know many cowboys. But there's the mountains and the Pacific Ocean." The conversation was launched again and the meal went along pleasantly until time for dessert. Kate rose and began clearing the table. Both children looked mystified and Harry sat with one arm hooked over the back of his chair.

"Is this all we're going to have?" Kate heard Raymond whisper as she disappeared with a load of dishes. The boy was again angrily hushed by his mother with an added threat he would be sent to the car if he said anything more until after dinner.

"Have you heard from Claud lately?" Ivan asked, trying to distract from the children's complaints.

"Not too long ago his wife wrote. He seems to have a good job with Midwestern Electric," his sister said.

"It ought to be a good place to work with Rural Electrification coming through soon."

"I hope it comes our way first, I got my stove and Frigidaire all picked out," Helga said. "How about you, Kate?"

Coming with hands full of pie she'd had to work loose from the pan, Kate laughed nervously. "I hadn't thought about that yet. I'm still trying to deal with the old . . . but not very successfully." She brought more coffee, then the milk pitcher, but noticed the children's glasses were still untouched. "Here I thought farm children drank lots of milk."

"Naw, we don't like milk. That's for the cats to drink. I want some water . . . please," said Raymond.

"I'll get it, Kate. Honest to goodness, these kids! Ivan, you wait till you and Kate have to put up with all this nonsense."

"We never drank milk either as kids," Ivan said. "I didn't get to liking it until I was away at school. It seemed to taste different poured from a glass bottle."

Harry said, "When I use any milk, which isn't very often, except on corn flakes or something, it's got to have all the cream off. Can't stand cream."

His wife agreed, "We have to draw too much milk out of the cows, I guess, to want to drink it. I wonder if Claud drinks milk poured from glass bottles now? Here he ended up being the city slicker and we always thought it would be you, Ivan."

Kate was absorbed with her own thoughts as she began on her piece of pie. More misconceptions and dillusions about farm life. No mother hen to brood her baby chickens and now to find that farmers don't drink milk or use cream. They don't even like it. She had noticed no milk on the Rockwell table but thought it was an economy.

It wasn't difficult for Kate to persuade Helga that they should just clear the table and she'd do the dishes later. The men had disappeared for the barn or the fields, so she asked Helga if she'd like to walk around outside and see the little that had been done with the flowers. Helga agreed but seemed only mildly interested. "Mom always worked on the flowers, I had all I could do to keep up the garden. That was my job." At noon when the fresh peas were passed, Kate acknowledged her pride in them. Helga asked Ivan if he remembered the huge garden she used to have.

The feud with Mattie Enders did not come up as Kate was afraid it might. If it did, she was going to remain silently dumb.

When the two women came back into the house and through the dining room, Helga stopped between the dining table with the cloth still on it and the marble-top table in the bay window. "I'm rather surprised you're using Mom's old table."

"Oh, I wouldn't have thought of discarding it. It's a lovely oak table and will seat twelve when all the leaves are in."

As though she hadn't heard Kate, Helga added without rancor, "Ivan always was the tightwad of the family." She turned to look behind her. "Where did you find this old marble-top table? I don't remember seeing it when we divided up things."

Kate flinched. Did Helga want it? She explained how she had proudly brought it down, step by step, from under the attic eaves.

"I was thinking about that old table at Christmas time when I ran across one of Mom's old candy recipes that said to turn the mixture out on a marble slab to cool."

Kate felt her throat tighten, but she found herself saying, "Do you want it? I doubt if I'll ever use it for making candy."

"I don't know what I'd do with it. I suppose I ought to take it for Mom's sake and keep it in the family. When you get something else to fill up the window, you might save it for me. I'll find someplace for it."

Something else to fill up the window! How could she replace it at any price? She forced down the lump in her throat. "If you want it, you'd better take it now before I get too attached to it."

"If I do it'll be easier to talk Ivan into buying something new, I bet." She winked knowingly at a silent, sober Kate and continued into the living room.

Kate tried to think of conciliatory words of protest but realized they would be ill-timed. Maybe she'd forget to take it. She straightened the bright chintz curtains at the window. They'd lose their soul without the table. She, too, continued on into the living room and sat down. Helga had picked up the

Sunday paper which they had brought along and for the moment was absorbed in it.

Shortly Harry came in from his tour around the farm with Ivan. "Say, we got seventy-five miles to go before chore time. Don't you think we better get started?"

"I suppose so. Where's the kids?"

"They went with Ivan to feed the chickens."

"Oh . . . I intended to have some ice cream and cookies before you go. Can you wait just a little longer till Ivan goes after the ice cream?" Kate asked hastily.

"No, Kate, thanks, we've had plenty. The kids will be hollering for ice cream cones before we get home anyway." Helga bundled the paper together and got up.

"I'll send some cookies along anyway. I'm afraid it was you who furnished the best part of the dinner." Kate tried to sound grateful but wished something – anything – would make Helga forget the table.

"That's all right. I didn't know how well you'd be settled yet and ready to fix a big dinner. Oh, Harry, take this table out and put it in the trunk. It'll fit in there, won't it?" Helga picked up the teapot and set it on the dining room table.

"Why are you taking that?" he asked, surprised.

"Kate wants me to take it. It's Mom's old table. Don't worry, I won't put it in the living room," she laughed. "It can go out there on the back porch where I've been wanting a table to set things on."

On the back porch! Kate, near tears, concentrated on finding a paper bag to put the cookies in, and another for the noodle kettle and the pie pan.

Harry walked gingerly through the door to the front porch, carrying the table. In a minute Kate heard the trunk lid slam. She cringed.

Ivan and the children came in through the back door and there was general commotion as they got their belongings together and prepared to start out. Kate said goodbyes and added as many little gracious remarks as she could manage, then waited on the front porch for them to make their departure. Ivan stood at the car, joking with the children through the back window.

Then the Clodfelter family started off down the lane. Everyone waved a last goodbye and Ivan walked smiling back to the porch.

The tears were already there. No use to hide them now. His expression changed abruptly. "What's this? You're not that sorry to see our relatives leave."

"Oh, Ivan, I'm just tired to death. I'm going to bed and sleep for a week." She slumped onto the stone wall and leaned her head against a post.

"Honey, it's more than that. What did she say to you? Or are you letting those little rascals get to you, the way they acted at the table?" He tipped her chin and looked soberly into her face.

She didn't want him to think it was that, badly as she thought the dinner had gone. She might as well tell him; he'd find it out sooner or later. She'd handled the situation so badly. "No, the table, why didn't she take it before I ever found it?" She sobbed against him.

"What table? Did she take that marble-top table!?!"

Kate nodded. "She said since her mother thought so much of it she ought to keep it in the family." Even in her distress she knew it sounded accusing.

"What the hell does she think we are?"

"She's . . . she's going to keep it on the back porch."

"I'm going after it. Harry said they had to stop at Onion Center for gas. I can catch them there."

"Oh, no, Ivan, please don't! It doesn't mean enough to cause life long friction over it."

He controlled his voice to a quiet pitch. "Kate, this is a sample of what I was afraid might happen in taking over a family farm. That's why when I bought this place, I wanted everything down in black and white so there would never be anything to squabble over. The three of us went over this farm, including everything in the house. At that time each of us had a chance to bargain for what we wanted, keepsakes or otherwise, then the rest went in the contract to be ours, yours and mine. Every old broken chair and onion crate. If that table meant a lot to her, we might consider letting her take it. But it doesn't. Actually, she wanted it because she could see you liked it. You might as well know Helga is a little like that." He lifted her face with both hands and kissed her gently. "Don't worry, darling, I'll use my best brotherly manner and be back with the table in a little while."

Kate watched the car disappear into the traffic on the highway, then slowly rose, walked into the house and through the living room into the bedroom and lay down on the soft comfort of the bed. She closed her eyes, trying to shut out thoughts of this day. It had been such a miserable failure. She had tried too hard to make a good impression. Why had she asked Helga if she wanted the table? Ivan going after it like she was a child! She was too tired to think about it and fell asleep.

Half an hour later she awakened when Ivan came softly to the door. When he saw she was awake he went to her and sat on the bed. She reached up and pulled him to her.

"The little table is back in the window where it belongs," he murmured. "There was no argument. I just explained how much it meant to you and she said, 'Well, for goodness sake take it back then.' She insisted she thought she was getting a piece of junk out of your way. Called me a tightwad," he grinned. "Just between you and me, I don't think she knows a good thing when she sees it."

"Junk, huh? And you a tightwad? Yes, I think she had her reckoning a little mixed up today. But I'm sure we'll be good friends in time. Now that I know she's so outspoken I'll defend myself. And she looks so much like you, how could I help but like her?"

CHAPTER 8

Picnic By The Lake

A COUPLE OF WEEKS AFTER the fiasco over the marble-top table, Kate asked Ivan over their 6 o'clock breakfast about his plans for the day.

"I'll be wheelhoeing onions in the field back by the lake for the next two or three days," he said. "They're looking good and I want them to stay that way."

"I take it a wheelhoe is a hoe on wheels?" Kate tried to imagine how such a contraption would look.

"Only one wheel," he laughed, "with little blades each side of it." He pointed his forefingers outward to an oblique angle. "It's lots of fun."

"I'll bet. If it's so much fun, how about me coming to join you around noon – with a picnic lunch?"

Ivan hesitated. "Well, I guess if you want. I never thought of having a picnic in the middle of a working day. But why not?" He shook his head slightly. "I'm sorry you have to think of things like this for some social life. I'd hoped we could make that weekend in Chicago by now."

"It's all right. You're the one who always works overtime. I should complain. Besides I love picnics and didn't think of it because I was bored."

"All right, but drive the car as far as you can, then I'll come meet you and carry the basket. Toot the horn."

Kate whipped through her morning work to leave ample time to prepare an extra special picnic lunch.

It was only a little past eleven when she dropped pieces of ice into a jar of lemonade, made from three squeezed lemons, loaded the rest of the food into what Ivan had said was his mother's old egg basket. Wednesday noon when neighbor women were coming in from their gardens or berry picking – or some of them would have been helping their husbands in the field – she was packing a picnic into the car. Three months she'd lived in this community and saw the people always working or hurrying to or from someplace. Didn't they ever stop and relax except at meals or in church?

Ivan was in the field next to the lake, going slowly up and down the rows, following the forward-then-backward motion of the two-bladed wheelhoe, making blacker the already black avenues between the points of green onions. He saw the car coming through the woods and watched her back around and park in the shade. He didn't care much for picnics, especially when mixed with wheelhoeing onions, but what she enjoyed he would also. It was with boyish delight he watched her alight from the car and toot the horn.

He saw her start out with the basket, take several steps, then kick off her shoes, pick them up and continue walking barefooted. He knew he should shout a warning but, mischievously, he'd let her discover them by herself. She moved along the edge of the field kicking up small clouds of dry, powdery muck behind her as she carried the covered basket and her shoes.

All at once, as he had anticipated, he heard her howl and jump away from the weeds at the edge of the ditch bank. Then she set the basket down and stooped to examine her legs and cautiously look into the weeds as though expecting to find a nest of hornets.

"What's the matter?" He was closer now.

"Something stung me!" She looked at him with distress and saw his amusement. "What kind of trap is this?"

"My nettles are trained to sting all barefooted people."

"Nettles! Now what?"

"This is a nettle." He kicked a tall green weed nearby.

"You devil, you were just waiting for me to walk into them? No sympathy from you, and ouch it stings."

He picked up the basket and laughingly put an arm around her. "It won't last long."

They chose a spot under a young willow tree right next to the lake's edge. Kate spread the bright cloth and began placing food upon it while Ivan went to the water to wash.

"Is it too early to eat?" she asked. "It isn't 12 o'clock yet."

"Gosh, no, let's eat. I'm starved – and thirsty."

After drinking a full glass of lemonade without stopping, he started on a sandwich of cold ham with fresh leaf lettuce from the garden. Then there was potato salad, baked beans still warm, and raspberries already sugared and juicy to finish up the meal. She had found enough berries for two in the tangle of bushes at the side of the garden.

"What a feast!" he said contentedly.

Kate so enjoyed watching Ivan and absorbing the peace and beauty of the setting that she almost forgot to eat. There were quiet little ripples on the lake, broken occasionally by a frog leaping for a lily pad. On the shore beneath the dipping willow a brief sandy slope disappeared into the water where they had been swimming a couple of times in the evenings. But Kate found the lake water still too cold to be enjoyable. Ivan said it was usually the Fourth of July before it was warm enough for most people. But since it was his only bathtub, besides a wash tub, he often went in while Kate sat nearby.

"Aren't we rich to have our own swimming pool and ice skating rink?" Kate hugged her knees with delight as Ivan lay back into the grass.

"The old swimming hole. Dad taught us kids to swim when we weren't much bigger than grasshoppers. He knew we weren't safe back here until we could swim. Mom always worried about us anyway. The water goes down pretty deep close to the edge."

"Just think of the job you'll have."

"We better have the kids first, don't you think?" He raised his head, propped it on an elbow and watched her as she put away the remains of the picnic and covered it with the cloth. "Dad had a good chance to sell the lake several years back to a man from Chicago who wanted to make a resort. Build a few cottages and fill in to make a wider and more shallow beach."

Kate thought of Emerald Lake, the resort they'd gone to Memorial Day night, where they'd had dinner at the Inn. It was teeming with people in a holiday mood. So different from the people the few other places they'd gone since she came. In Richland and Morriston on Saturday nights the crowds were mostly farm people, many of them whole families standing on street corners or in front of the stores, visiting with other families or waiting to go to the movie. Ivan had said the people at the lake were cottagers who came from the cities for weekends and holidays.

"No, we won't ever commercialize this lake, just keep it for ourselves and the neighbors – swimming, fishing, boating, ice skating . . ."

"You forgot putting-up-ice-off-of."

"Also picnicing. Speaking of ice reminds me you'll have to get more out, right after you come up from the field. It was just about gone in the ice box when I made the lemonade. Of course, I let the pan run over again. In fact it was running all over the porch when I discovered it."

Having their own private little ice house with the blocks of ice buried deep in sawdust was another wonderment to Kate. since there had been no one living on the farm for the past winters when it was time to put up the ice, neighbors had hauled it in and stored it away as they always had. Now those same neighbors came to the little ice house beside the orchard and dug out a block at a time for their refrigerators or to make ice cream.

"Toward the end of summer it isn't so nice back here. The water gets pretty scummy around the edges. The ditch doesn't keep it moving fast enough, I guess."

"You mean the ice we use is taken off that kind of water?" She looked closely at the small piece left in her cup.

Ivan laughed. "The scum is gone again by wintertime. I guess between the sun and the freezing it gets sterilized. Anyway we've always used it and nobody ever got sick from it."

Kate lay on her back a few feet away from Ivan. "Do you suppose your grandparents, aunts and uncles had picnics back here? I'll bet if they did they had fried chicken."

"Actually I guess they had chicken about every day when the other meat was gone and they couldn't butcher in warm weather. My mother said her mother used to flour the chicken and put it in lard in the big black skillet the night before so it was ready to start frying as soon as the fire was built. Then they'd have it for breakfast. Mom seldom ate fried chicken after I knew her – sick of it, I guess."

"That was Grandma Elizabeth who fried the chicken?"

"Grandpa Tallock's wife."

"Have you got time to tell me about him?"

★ ★ ★ ★

In the spring of 1849 Grandpa Cary and Uncle Alex (twin to Leander) came to Indiana for the orphaned Stangland children who had survived the winter looking well and reasonably content. Even though years earlier John Cary had said he would never ride a train or anything that moved faster than a horse can run, he relented and took the children to New York by train. Grandma Cary couldn't face such a trip and had to depend on Rosetta 12, to mother the little ones along the way.

Baby Frankie, now well past a year old and weaned from Mrs. Young's nurturing breast, was walking and beginning to talk. Grandpa Cary was quite taken with him. "Well, if that little feller doesn't remind me of his mother at that age," he said huskily. "Bright as a button and tow-colored hair."

When the eight children reached Kendall, several families asked to take one or more of the children to raise, especially after they saw what well-behaved and good-looking children they were. It was decided that Frankie would stay with Rosetta at the Cary's. He had already become Uncle Alex's shadow and continued to follow him at every opportunity until Alex married six years later.

Mary Elizabeth was taken by the Cook family, near Morton. Jack was raised by the Wilson family on Norway road. Maria joined a doctor's family in Carleton. However, the children saw each other and their grandparents frequently.

Eleazer worked hard through the summer at every job he could find and by fall had enough money, with a little help from the Carys, to enroll at Brockport College to begin his career in medicine.

Tallock worked on the Cary farm for his Grandpa and Uncle Alex. But he couldn't forget the Indiana farm – his home. He thought about the fishing, the trapping, the hunting he'd formerly enjoyed. Each year he kept hoping to make a trip back there, but he could not save any money since he and Bela were expected to work on the farm to help support themselves and the younger children. The grandparents were aging and no longer able to do hard work.

In the early fall of his twenty-first year, after most of the harvest was in, Tallock told his grandparents he was going to walk to the farm in Indiana. There would be taxes to pay and things to see to before the farm was declared deserted. They were against it, but Uncle Alex took Tallock's side and said it would be good for him.

Sometimes on the long walk Tallock camped out in his small bed roll. Other times he was offered a bed in someone's barn after helping a farmer milk or pick apples. Occasionally he was taken as a vagrant, a beggar, and sent on his way with angry words. But finally he reached Noble County in Indiana where people recognized the name Stangland, remembered the orphaned family of children, and treated him to their best.

Tallock found the home farm buildings in poor condition. Time and the weather had taken its toll. Windows had blown out, letting in rain and debris. The roof leaked in several places; mice, squirrels and birds had invaded the whole house. But hardest to endure was nothing tangible, it was the ghosts of memories that hovered over him when he tried to sleep. After the first night he took his bed roll along with the best of the covers left in the house, and went back to sleep in the woods by the lake. It had been his favorite haunt in years past when he wrestled with bouts of anger or despair. The quiet ripples on the lake had calmed him and absorbed his tears.

He visited neighbors to ask if they knew of anyone who wanted to buy enough of the land to pay his taxes and soon made such a transaction. Then as he had promised his grandparents, he headed back to New York before winter set in.

On the way back, with lots of time to think, Tallock devised a plan. While waiting at the courthouse to pay the taxes, he had overheard a conversation between a man and some county official. He was having a time, the trustee complained, finding a suitable teacher to take a school – the name of which Tallock didn't recognize. Two women teachers had married and had to quit, now he was looking for a man.

Why couldn't I teach school, Tallock wondered, and earn some money to get the farm going again? He began to build on the idea. Maybe he could take some extra courses during the winter, perhaps at Brockport where Leazer was in college. With an income he could build himself a little house. Maybe Bela would come back with him and help. The farm belonged to all of them, his brothers and sisters, too. Leazer wasn't interested except to get money to go to medical school. Mother was a schoolteacher when she met Pa, straight out of Norway, Tallock remembered. In fact she taught him to speak English. It never occurred to Tallock to teach school. But he had always done well in his classes, so why couldn't he teach if it was the means to go back to running their farm? The two occupations ought to fit together well; farm in summer and teach in winter.

So it was that brothers Tallock and Bela set out walking to Indiana the following spring. The trip was shorter and the house less lonesome with two of them to share it. They cleaned up enough of the house to live in and closed off the rest.

Again Tallock searched for a buyer and sold a fifty-acre plot for a team of horses and $50 to buy seed and necessary equipment. His father's old plow would serve them for awhile.

After the spring crops were in, Tallock began scouting for a school needing a teacher for fall. All the nearby schools were already set with returning teachers. Tallock became discouraged. Maybe teaching jobs were not so easy to find after all, even though he had taken teaching courses and read the books professors at the college had recommended. He also carried with him letters of recommendation.

In mid-August a Mr. Murphy, trustee of Washington Township, called on Tallock and offered him the Indian Creek school. However it was so far from where he lived in Noble Township, Tallock had to turn it down.

A few days later, Mr. Murphy returned. "How would you feel about boarding over there near the school through the week with a family who has eight children, most of them in the school? The Abrams are a nice family and said they could find room for you."

★ ★ ★ ★

Ivan rolled over on his side to look at Kate, who had been listening intently. "They had eight children and the oldest was named Elizabeth," he grinned.

"Uh-oh. That was your grandmother's name."

CHAPTER 9

Tallock

KATE OPENED THE DOOR to the shiny new mailbox on the wooden post Ivan had cemented in, and drew out the daily newspaper. Folded in it was just one letter. It was from Tommy. She fairly ran down the lane for home in order to open it. Mostly she only heard from her brother through her parents' weekly letters, but once in awhile he wrote. It was usually written on a dull night in some hotel too small to have a bar or gathering place where he could nurse a couple of drinks for a whole evening of conversation with friends, often those he'd just met.

She read and reread the letter, then dreamily placed it back in the envelope to read to Ivan at noon. But at noon Ivan was in the house only long enough to eat, then was off to Richland. She hadn't even asked him why he needed to go. So the letter waited until evening when they had both settled in the porch swing, their favorite sitting-together place, late June evening surrounding them.

"Dear Little Sister," she read.

> "Well, here I am in a little berg called Sutter Creek, California. I drove out of my way to get here because the name has been beckoning to me. Gold was discovered near here at Sutter's Mill in 1848 by a James Marshall. Before dark I drove around a bit (quite a bit, in fact) on a lovely winding road through vineyards and past a small winery. There are still many manifestations of the past gold mining operations. The hills fairly sing of history and romance. Now I am ensconced in a tiny tourist room in a village that goes to bed early. A pleasant breeze blows over me and billows the curtains as I write to you.
>
> How I miss you and our frequent exchange of confidences. Will your marriage and the distance that separates us end it? I hope not. News of you gets to me through

Mother and Dad when I'm home. But, as you know, that is not regularly.

I am sure you must be just the happiest bride in Indiana, a state I've never been in. I promise to yield to a yearning to visit there soon.

Participating in and enjoying your lovely wedding and seeing how happy you two are together, almost makes me matrimony-minded. (Please note – *almost.*) I suppose if I were to find the right girl I would have eagerly approached the altar before this. Or perhaps I haven't looked very hard. It would mean an office job, if I were to have any stability in a marriage. And I am really quite content as a traveling salesman. So far I've found no reason to change.

Do take care of that wonderful man of yours. He's a prince!"

It was signed, "Love always, Tommy."

"So, I'm a prince, am I?" Ivan laughed. "Well, this prince doesn't write letters like that. I'm mostly the 'How are you? I am fine and I hope you are the same,' kind of letter writer."

"I don't know that." Kate snuggled close to him. "Fortunately we've never been separated long enough for you to write me a letter. Tommy has quite a flair for writing. He won some awards in high school and college. He probably could write for publication if he worked at it. But I imagine it is too solitary an occupation to suit him."

"How much older is he than you – two or three years?"

"Just two. We had so much fun as children. He'd always want to go around the neighborhood selling something." Kate laughed remembering. "He'd usually sell it, too, if Mom or Dad didn't catch us first. I always had to tag along and carry the goods or pull the wagon."

They sat silently and gently swinging for a few moments and listened to the mourning doves' last laments of the day. "I miss him so much," she said finally.

He laid his head against hers. "I know you do – and your parents. Poor little Katie so far from home."

She sat up straight and shook her head, "Oh, fiddle dee dee, I'm a big girl now. Tell me the rest of the story about Grandpa Tallock and get my mind off my family."

"Even if it's a sad story?"

Kate hesitated, "Yes, even if it's a sad story."

★ ★ ★ ★

Tallock took the teaching job at Indian Creek School in Washington Township even though he didn't get his license until late November. He stayed with the James Abrams' family from Monday evening until Friday morning each week the school was in session.

Since Tallock had always lived in a large family, being in a home with eight children didn't bother him. In their large house he had an attic room to himself and ate well. In fact when he went home weekends and told Bela what all he'd had to eat, his brother was envious. But Bela was spending time away from home, too, keeping company with Caroline Richmond who lived on a neighboring farm. They were married the following spring and moved in with her parents. But Bela continued to farm his share of the Stangland acres and helped Tallock.

During that summer Tallock, with Bela's help, built a small cabin for himself apart from the old dilapidated buildings. He'd been able to save some money during the winter even after buying himself clothes more suited to his job of teaching.

He enjoyed the children in the one-room eight grades school, helping them learn, playing with them at recess, hearing their complaints, helping if he could. Tallock was a strict disciplinarian but fair and understanding.

He tried to treat the Abrams' children as family while in their home, switching to teacher only at school.

Elizabeth (known as Libby) hadn't planned to attend school another year, but her mother told her that a new teacher might have more to offer her. Besides, she needed to get the younger children there safely since Tallock left early to build a fire and warm the school. Libby was easily convinced to spend the day in class with the personable new young teacher, not tall but strong-muscled. Above brown eyes in a gentle face often faintly smiling, he had a shock of unruly black hair. Libby was amused at his familiar gesture of trying to put it back in place.

Tallock often visited with Elizabeth at recess since she was the oldest in school and often alone. He asked her opinion on different aspects of the daily activities. She was wise and sensible. At home he avoided her as much as possible to keep their relationship on a teacher-pupil basis.

But toward spring of his second year of teaching it was increasingly hard to keep his feelings under wraps. Trees were beginning to bud, the frogs in the pond were mating and everything encouraged love, especially the brown-haired, brown-eyed girl who sat in a back corner discreetly watching him when she thought he didn't notice.

On the next to the last day of school he said in teacherly fashion, "Libby, can you stay for a few minutes after school or do you need to see the children home?"

"I'll stay. They can run on home. They usually beat me by a mile anyway."

He waited till the room emptied, then sat at his desk looking down for several moments before he raised his eyes to meet hers. "Libby, do you plan to attend school next year?" He continued before she had time to answer. "I think I've taught you about as much as I can. From now on reading books will do you as much good as my teaching." A frown of disappointment crossed her face and he quickly added. "Oh, I don't mean that I don't want you here." He paused again fidgeting in his chair. "In fact . . . having you here is beginning to mean too much to me." He slowly rose and came around to stand in front of the bench where she sat. "Libby, I've fallen in love with you. May I keep company with you this summer?"

Surprised, she looked up at him for a few silent moments, then stood and held out her hand to him, brown eyes twinkling and dimples forming in her rosy cheeks. "I'd like that," she said shyly.

Tallock took her hand in both of his, held it tightly for an instant, then raised it to his lips and finally rubbed it against his cheek.

The summer went by with Tallock spending almost every Sunday after church at the Abrams' household for dinner, after which the two of them went for long rides in his buggy. Or they took walks in the woods on the Stangland farm where one day, on a large beech tree, he carved their initials and surrounded it with a heart. From then on it was always referred to as "our tree." In the winter they went in the sleigh, bells jangling, to events at either his church or hers.

The following spring on April 18, 1861 just after Abraham Lincoln became president and the Civil War began, Tallock and Libby were married. The bride was 20, the groom 29. For the occasion Tallock bought himself a fashionable long beige linen jacket to wear as he took the vows beside his lovely bride in her self-made wedding gown.

They lived in the cabin Tallock had built for himself. Libby found pleasure in fixing up their little home with bright curtains, table covers and the quilt she had made. Tallock was delighted with his new wife's warmth and charm along with her daily cooking and baking. Both of them loved to go fishing and often on a late summer evening they'd walk to the lake with their fish poles. Usually the evening ended with love-making beneath their special beech tree.

Libby was anxious for her mother to come see her new home but her mother was pregnant and nearly bedfast with swollen legs. "As big as she is she must be going to have twins," Libby remarked to Tallock.

It was only a few days later when her brother, Stephen, came with the news: "We've got twin brothers, James and William."

The babies were small but thriving and Barbara Abrams was up and caring for them after a few days. By the time the twins were ten days old, the mother felt equal to a trip to visit her daughter and see their house.

Libby and her parents with the twins enjoyed the day together. But the trip in the spring wagon, so they could take more things to Libby than in the buggy, was harder on the mother then either parent anticipated.

By the time James Abrams got his wife home she was bleeding heavily. The doctor could not be reached in time and before morning she was so weakened nothing could save her. The twin boys, as well as the rest of the children, were left motherless. And Barbara Woodcock Abrams was laid to rest in Stringtown Cemetery, Washington Township.

The twins were put on cow's milk since nearby nursing mothers could not be found soon enough. Their under developed digestive systems couldn't tolerate it and they soon died one after the other. James was just 13 days old and William lived 24 days. They were buried in little graves beside their mother.

Libby tried to help at home as much as she could but was in the early throes of her own pregnancy and suffering from nausea. A young woman in her twenties was hired to care for the children and run the Abrams' household. Before long James Abrams married her and they began another family before he died three years later.

Following the year after the twins death, Lenora Alice was born to Tallock and Libby. She was a beautiful baby and as sweet natured as a child could be. Libby cherished her.

Fifteen months later a boy was born. He was named for his Uncle Bela who earlier that year had died of tuberculosis at age 26, leaving Carolyn and two very young children.

During Bela's illness Eleazer was nearing his final months of medical school; he prescribed for his brother by letter the latest known care for tuberculosis – fresh air, rest and nourishing food – but the disease was too far along.

★ ★ ★ ★

As Ivan told this part of Tallock's life to Kate she sighed heavily. "So many deaths! What a tragic life poor Grandpa and Grandma must have led."

"Well, I'm sorry to say it didn't end there," Ivan said, dreading to continue. "When Lenora and little Bela were still very little, under three years old, a dreaded disease called 'the flux' swept through the Midwest and struck down hundreds of children. Bloody flux, they called it, diarrhea and vomiting, I guess, and no way to stop it. Again, both children died very close together. Little Nora just past two years old, ten days before Bela at seven months."

"Oh, no!" Kate cried. "How did parents keep their sanity through such sorrow?"

Ivan sighed and shook his head. "My mother said they just had to console themselves and each other by saying it was 'God's will.' Anyway, the grandparents managed to go on with life, had eight more children and built a big, new house. Part of our back porch and cellar is some of it.

"The 600 acres dwindled further when Grandpa's sisters and brothers sold off their shares but he was able to buy some of their lots to add to his own and the farm became the present 160 acres.

"Through the years Grandpa Tallock continued to teach, 20 years altogether. I'm not sure which schools, there were several closer by than the

Indian Creek school and he must have taught at some of them. There's Poplar school, Wild Cat, Bug Island, Little Lake, Stultz, Burr Oak . . ."

In spite of her tears, Kate laughed. "They were colorful names to be sure."

"Yes, and I remember my mother telling about the winter Grandma's youngest sister, Flora, stayed with them. She was a girl of 15 or 16 and they were worried about her getting involved with the 'wild bunch' over at Bug Island school."

"You went to one of those *wild* schools didn't you?"

"That was Poplar, the best of them, of course. I've lots of pleasant memories from that school. It's still there. We'll go visit it sometime."

"Let's do. But go on with your story. With so many children and relatives did grandma and grandpa continue to prosper?"

"They must have or at least their relatives must have thought they had money. Leazer wrote asking to borrow $100 for a cadaver for his final medical tests. Several cousins in Norway wrote asking for passage money to emigrate to America. Grandpa Tallock also sent money each month to help support a Christian college at Mermon, Indiana.

"However each fall he gave in to his once-a-year fling, hunting deer in the north woods. In November of 1880 the hunt took him to Wisconsin, where he shot and wounded a deer. He chased it until he was near exhaustion. The next day, weary and sick, he managed to get to the depot and on the train for home. But by the time he got to a depot just 15 miles from here, he was unconscious. No one knew who he was and he was taken to a nearby home.

"Finally someone identified him and Grandma was summoned. A neighbor drove her there, but the doctor didn't think it advisable to move him in the severe weather they were having. So she stayed through the winter to care for him with a still-nursing baby at her breast.

"So again," said Ivan, "seven Stangland children spent the winter as orphans on this place." Kate shuddered. "The oldest was Aunt Grace, 16. Somewhere in those old letters upstairs is a short note Grandma wrote to her children just before Christmas. As I remember, it says, 'Go to Uncle 'Nealous's for Christmas dinner. Be sure the boys wear extra overalls so they won't catch cold. Mama misses you.' "

"How pathetic," Kate murmured.

Ivan continued, "When the first spring sunshine warmed things up a little, the doctor permitted Grandpa to be taken home in the spring wagon. He declared that if he didn't get home he'd die of homesickness anyway; he wanted so much to see the children.

"It must have been a happy month for the family being all together again. Grandpa was bedfast most of the time, but he allowed the children to take him for short rides on the big hand sled while there was still snow on the ground. Other times he sat in the warm sunshine wrapped in a blanket.

"Uncle Leazer wrote that he was coming and would be his brother's private physician and make him well and strong again. But that didn't happen. Grandpa died April 10, 1881 at the age of 49 after 20 years of marriage. The oldest of the boys was Uncle Omar. He was 11."

"How very, very sad," Kate said as they sat in silence for a few moments, swinging slightly. "Did you remember your Grandmother?"

"Oh, yes, I remember her well. She was solemn. Why wouldn't she be? Quiet, soft spoken, always busy, even when she was sitting down – knitting socks or darning them or peeling potatoes or fruit." Ivan chuckled, "Every time I open the cellar door I remember the wonderful smell of apples they used to store down there to last the winter. We always stored a few crates, but they had bushel upon bushel stacked up there to eat fresh and use in applesauce and pies. And always there was a covered crock of applebutter which they made outdoors each fall in a big copper-lined iron kettle.

"We used to come here for applebutter making – Thanksgivings and Christmases. She kept a well-ordered household and peaceful surroundings. She also apparently liked to read aloud, or else she considered it education, because Mom said they used to sit around her on the floor and she would read to them from *Harper's Weekly* or the *Youths' Companion.*"

"I'll bet she was a good cook."

"Yes. Although the aunts did most of it after I can remember. They sort of ran the household it seemed to me; Grandma kind of stayed in the background and filled in where needed. I'm sure she is the one who made the sugar cookies, though. The jar was always full of them for the taking. Those and the little sugar pears in the orchard I remember so well. They were just a tiny little pear but so sweet and juicy. The tree is gone from the orchard now, unfortunately." He nodded his head in that direction.

"And I can't even make sugar cookies," Kate pouted.

Ivan laughed. "You're not a grandmother yet."

"There were always extra people at Grandma's, nieces, nephews, cousins, aunts, uncles, grandchildren, staying for a week or a month. Sometimes a whole school season."

"When did the onion raising start?"

"That wasn't till after Grandpa died that the muck was drained sufficiently to grow good crops."

"How did they manage the farm work when the boys were so young?"

"They had a good hired hand. At least Aunt Nell must have thought so. She married him and after a few years they moved to Iowa and prospered there. In fact they raised a woman doctor and an engineer son."

The last of daylight faded as husband and wife continued to swing gently back and forth enmeshed in time and the events which had happened on their farm, so much of it tragic.

Kate finally spoke, "I hope I'm never put to any of those tests of fortitude. I don't see myself as a Susan or a Libby. Of course, you have already passed your test . . . with the death of your parents." She wrapped an arm around his chest and laid her head on his shoulder.

Ivan didn't comment for several moments, not wanting to think about the painful memory so close to him. Then he closed his arm around her and said cheerfully, "Except for that, the Stanglands mostly died of old age. Grandma was 84. Great Aunt Rosetta lived to 90 after having 13 children and they'd celebrated their seventieth wedding anniversary. I think we'll take after her."

"Thirteen children! Seventy years of marriage! We better look for that beech tree back in the woods," Kate quipped.

Teacher's License.

STATE OF INDIANA,
Noble County, } SS.
Nov 28 1868

Mr N A Stangland having presented satisfactory evidence of good moral character, and having been duly examined as to his ability to impart instruction, I hereby License him to teach a Common School in this County for a period of 6 Months from the date hereof.

75 to 80 per cent.	Six Months, or Third Grade.
80 to 90 per cent.	One Year, or Second Grade.
90 to 100 per cent.	Two Years, or Third Grade,

Grade No. .... T. M. Eells Examiner.

CHAPTER 10

Sunday School Lesson

AFTER HEARING A HISTORY, brief as it was, of the Stangland farm, Kate was awed by a sense of duty. Was she up to carrying on in the footsteps of those brave women who came before her on this farm and suffered unbearable losses and heartaches? Shouldn't she be doing something more than just tending her house and garden?

For a small beginning, her opportunity came the following week by way of a call from a Mrs. Verbank. Kate remembered meeting the tall, solemn, middle-aged woman on one of the Sundays she and Ivan had attended the little country church where Ivan had belonged since childhood and his great grandfather had been a charter member. The caller asked Kate if she'd take the nursery class for Sunday school on the following Sunday. Neither she nor the substitute could be there, she said. Serena Rockwell had suggested Kate.

With little hesitation Kate accepted. But later, as she thought about the class, she got a little nervous. Mrs. Verbank hadn't mentioned what kind of lesson she was supposed to teach; there must be some sort of guide to follow. But for six or eight little children, Kate reasoned, she could keep them interested in something of value. After all in her growing up years, she had been hired several times to care for children. And in college, she had taken a course in child development.

On Sunday morning Kate left Ivan in the young marrieds' class and went to the corner of the one-room church where the little red chairs were gathered around in a semicircle and were already filling with youngsters brought over by parents or older siblings. All were dressed in their shiny best.

Most of them were shy, facing the new young teacher. Kate's heart reached out to them; she was sure she would enjoy the hour. She was perturbed, however, that they were meeting in a corner with no partition whatever, only a few feet away from other classes grouped together. Whatever she said could be heard by anyone who listened. When Mr. Lowe, the jolly, round-faced superintendent, came along to give out the papers and to see if there were anything else she needed, Kate asked if it would be possible to take the children out on the side lawn since it was such a warm day.

"Yes, sure, Mrs. Anderson, if you think you can handle them by yourself out there. The highway's close, you know, but some of the teachers take their classes outdoors on nice days."

So Kate told her little group of seven that they were going to have Sunday school outdoors that morning, and that they must go out quietly by the side door nearest them. She settled her class into a half-sunny, half-shady spot near the church away from the highway. Most of them were already warming up to her friendliness.

She glanced briefly at the papers that had been handed to her to pass out. On the front was a picture of Samuel and the old priest, Eli. The story of Samuel hearing God's voice and thinking it was Eli calling him seemed very difficult to explain to pre-school children, but apparently that was to be their lesson for the day. The thought of a strange voice in the night would be but frightening to them. And those people in long robes so different from people they knew. No, she'd go on with her original idea. She decided to lay the papers aside and pass them out just before they adjourned.

"Do you know why we came outside today?" she smilingly began. "So we can see better the things that God has made." The children looked around them as though it were a new idea to them. "He makes the trees grow, the soft grass where we are sitting, the nice white clouds high up in the sky." For a moment they all looked upward. "God has made them all, so that we may have a beautiful world to live in. At home He makes our gardens grow and the berries ripen and turn red. But He expects us to help Him by hoeing and keeping the weeds out, by watering them sometimes when there isn't enough rain. God means for us to work with Him and to help."

All the children, except one little girl who could hardly be past two, were listening. Kate gently took the child on her lap and went on talking.

"When God put people on this earth, He wanted them to love each other, not to fight and quarrel, but to help each other. He wants little boys and girls to take turns when they are playing and to share instead of quarreling over their toys." She talked to them softly a little while longer, until she could see they were beginning to get restless – little bodies that were used to constant activity.

"Now let's fold our hands, like this, close our eyes and bow our heads and be very quiet while we say a little thank-you prayer to God, then we'll play a game."

Except for a couple of very shy youngsters, they folded their hands obediently and repeated after her, "Thank you, God, for our beautiful world and all you do for us."

Kate then took two handkerchiefs from her purse and tied them together into a soft ball. "In this game you're going to help me learn your names. See, I say, 'Helen,' and throw the ball to her. Helen says someone else's name and throws the ball to that boy or girl. Remember, God wants us to take turns, so let's give everyone a chance to toss the ball."

The game was so simple even the smallest could enter into it. When they were seated again, Kate told in simple language about God's plan for birds to build nests and squirrels to gather nuts – just as people fill their cellars with supplies to last through the winter. Some of the more talkative children added their own thoughts.

The hour passed pleasantly. None of them had even attempted to run away from the group. Noticing that the time was almost up, Kate picked up the bag she'd brought along and told them she'd baked some cookies just for them. They had been such good, good children. They clapped with delight as Kate went around the circle and laid a yellow cookie, the shape of a duck, on each out-stretched hand. "Let's wait until each of you has one, then we'll pretend it is a whole meal and say thank you to God before we eat." She then shared with them a prayer from her earliest memory:

Thank you for the world so sweet.
Thank you for the food we eat.
Thank you for the birds that sing.
We thank you, God, for everything.
Amen.

As they ate their cookies, one little girl with long, dark curls said, "I'm going to say that blessing at home sometime." Her name was Elizabeth Verbank. She was apparently Mrs. Verbank's granddaughter.

When the other classes adjourned, the children ran to find their families. Some of them would go home; others would stay with their parents through church. Pleased with her first experience in teaching Sunday school, Kate rejoined Ivan.

After church as they walked to their car, greetings all around, one of the young parents whispered to Kate, "Jerry wishes you were their teacher every Sunday."

But next day, late in the morning, after Kate had the Monday washing on the line, she got a call from Mrs. Verbank. She thanked Kate for *entertaining* her Sunday school class while she had to be gone. She didn't expect to have to desert them again soon. "Frank Lowe should have told you that the lesson and the memory verse were on the Sunday school paper. I usually read it to them and explain it. But Elizabeth told me you got by anyway. You went out on the lawn and had a party."

Rebuffed and chagrined, Kate hesitated. Should she apologize or attempt to explain? "I hope it didn't seem like only a party," Kate said finally. "I wasn't prepared for the lesson on the paper even though I knew it was there. We talked about God and the things He'd made that we could see. Then when they got restless, we played a little game."

"Yes, I know they get awfully fidgety. I have to get real firm with them sometimes to make them sit through the lesson. But I realize it's hard when you haven't had much experience with children. Now, don't think I'm criticizing you, Mrs. Anderson. It's good to find a young woman in the church willing to take over. If any of the parents complain about the children not getting their Bible lesson, I'll just tell them you took over on the spur of the moment and weren't prepared."

Kate tried to think of the right words to protest, but decided against it. "Thanks," she said briefly. "Goodbye."

Seething with frustration, Kate hung up the receiver, spied her knitting on the stand under the wall telephone and grabbed it. She went out to the porch swing and began knitting furiously as she swung rapidly back and forth.

It wasn't fair, not only to her but to those dear little children, pushing Bible stories on them in a meaningless way. Did she want her children to be born and grow up in a community where so much of the thinking was narrow-minded and stereotyped? Could she and Ivan alone give their hoped-for children the background desired for them? She thought of the silly feud with Mattie Enders (whatever it was about), of Michelle Rockwell's unhappiness, and Helga and Harry's children who hated milk and salads. She added stitch after speedy stitch to the recently-begun afghan.

CHAPTER 11

Women's Work

IN SPITE OF THE HEAT, a small army of onion weeders invaded the fields. Wheelhoeing could no longer reach all the weeds. The rows needed to be cleaned out by hand, a section at a time. With Ivan working along side of them, each weeder straddled one row and reached for the weeds on a row on either side of him. Most of the workers were of high school age, but some were younger. They came from nearby small towns or from other farms and were not presently needed at home. This group had just finished the Rockwell fields, when Ivan hired them. He picked them up each morning at the Onion Center filling station. Ivan would like to have kept the Rockwell children in the group, but they could not be spared to hire out.

Most of the weeders were good workers; others (not always the youngest) weren't earning their hourly wage. But it wasn't easy to find weeders since it was the busy season and no one wanted to weed onions if there was any other job available. Ivan treated them well, with brief rest periods around the windmill pump or in the shade at the edge of the fields, or by the lake when they worked in that field. Each brought along his lunch and they sat together in a shady spot to eat.

That hour was the only time Ivan left them, just long enough to go in and eat his own dinner. He usually asked Kate to make the weeders a pail of iced tea to go with what they had brought in their dinner pails – pails that had formerly held lard or syrup. They were a noisy group during the early part of the day, but at quitting time they were sober and quiet with streaks of perspiration through the masks of muck.

Kate wondered what kind of an onion weeder she would have made at that age – or even now. Why couldn't she go out and work with them part of the day? Their friendly bantering, Ivan in the midst of them, made her feel left out and lonesome. She could work a few hours and still get the meals, even if she had to neglect some of the house cleaning until the weeding was done.

Perhaps it would help her forget the heat, so humid and different than the climate in the Northwest. The heat wave started right after the Fourth of July. From morning to evening her damp clothes clung to her and her hair drooped. Most evenings they went for a brief swim; but it was short-lived refreshment. And Kate never felt clean from the lake water, so she followed the swim with a sponge bath. They went to bed at dark and Ivan slept from sheer weariness while Kate moved from place to place trying to find the coolest spot. Sometimes she ended up on the floor in front of an open door.

Redecorating the upstairs now, as she had planned, wasn't possible. It was like an oven up there. No overnight company was expected anyway. Her parents had hoped to make the trip to Indiana but wrote they wouldn't be able to come till at least fall. She had heard no more from Tommy, but it wasn't likely he'd be in the area yet. It was plain to Kate that she and Ivan wouldn't be taking any trips, much as she'd like to escape the heat. There just wasn't time nor money. The chores had to be done day after day every day of the week. Even though discouraged, she had no right to complain, it was Ivan who did them. Onion weeding just might make her feel more like a partner.

That evening at supper Kate smiled mysteriously across the table at her husband. "Can you use another weeder tomorrow?"

"Why? Did someone call?"

"No, but I'm coming out and try it – part of the day at least."

Ivan laid down his fork and frowned at her. "You are not going to weed onions."

Kate was hurt and revealed it. "And why not? I'm not that delicate just because I was raised in town. I rather enjoy weeding in the garden."

"Honey, it's hot dirty work. You aren't used to it like those toughened kids."

"At least it might help me forget the heat for awhile to get out there with someone to talk to and laugh with."

Ivan returned bleakly to his plate. "Come on out then if that is what you think you want."

He went back to his chores without referring to the subject again. As he wearily milked the cows, the heat of the barn and depressing thoughts closed in on him. His wife going out to weed onions for companionship! Where was his idea of having a *different* kind of farm life leading? Maybe he hadn't gotten the idea across to Kate. If only she could realize that this is the busy season for farmers, not like it will be the year around.

Next morning Kate got up with Ivan at 4 o'clock and tried to hurry through a minimum of housework, at the same time thinking ahead to dinner preparation. She would wash the breakfast dishes and the milking things while Ivan went after the weeders. The rushing about made her feel dizzy. Even in the early morning the air was humid. After making an early pot of coffee, she wanted only a few sips of it. Was she regretting her decision to go out and weed onions? She tried to believe that if the little she could do would help get the job done sooner, she'd stick it out with the rest.

Even though feeling bilious, she forced down breakfast and felt a little better. After the dishes were done, she put on a pair of Ivan's overalls, hitched up to size, and an old long-sleeved blouse. She then added her wide-brimmed garden hat. She was ready to go when Ivan returned with the hands in Rockwells' pickup truck, which Rocky insisted they use whenever it was needed.

The weeders stared at Kate and said little as she cheerfully joined them. She was proud of being able to keep up with the experienced weeders and was doing a good job, too, even though aware of the dirt that dug under her fingernails and the hot sun on her back. By the end of the second hour when Ivan announced time to knock off for a drink of water and a few minutes rest, Kate got to her feet slowly and cautiously. She was dizzy and didn't want Ivan to see her staggering. He treated her no more personally than the rest and she wouldn't have wanted him to. She saw him looking anxiously at her and smiled an I'm-fine back at him.

While the rest of the weeders gathered around the windmill she went into the house. Was this the house she thought so hot yesterday? She got a glass of iced tea from the ice box, then remembered the drip pan hadn't been emptied. Finally she laid her head on her arms at the table for a few minutes. She was glad Ivan didn't come in. Heavens above, another hour and a half before time to come in and get dinner. But she'd never had a job yet that the first day wasn't the hardest.

Back in the field again Ivan noticed that the figure under the big flowered hat a few weeders away from him was not as talkative as she had been earlier. It slowed him down just worrying about her. He worried about all the weeders; in this kind of weather one of them might be overcome with the heat. It was shy of eleven o'clock when he told Kate it was the time she'd planned to quit. He watched her walking slowly to the back door.

As soon as Kate entered the kitchen she sank into a chair and fanned herself with her hat for a few moments. Then she took off her blouse and washed with cool water. Every minute counted. She decided not to cook the potatoes already laid out to peel; they'd have left over potato chips with the wieners, along with radishes and the tapioca pudding she'd made the night before. She remembered the kerosene lamps that had to be filled before night and thought of their dirty chimneys needing to be washed.

She managed to have dinner ready by the time Ivan came in. He too looked tired, hot and haggard. They ate almost in silence. Kate put away the perishables and thankfully lay down on the bed. Ivan was already on the davenport which she kept covered these days with a makeshift spread to guard it against the dirt from his clothes.

It seemed but a few minutes before Ivan came to the bedroom door, hat in hand and ready to go again. "Don't you think you should stay in this afternoon?"

"Of course I'm not going to quit on half a day's trial. I feel rested now," she lied. She followed him out, trying not to think of the dishes still on the table that would have to be washed before supper.

From the beginning of the afternoon she worked in a daze with nothing to say and barely managing to keep up. If she could just get rid of that giddy feeling. Hot sun, and she'd been in lots of it, never made her feel like this. It must be the change in climate. At the end of the first round she got weakly to her feet with the rest, who had finished and were now stretching, ready to begin on return rows. Ivan was helping some of the slower weeders catch up. She took off her hat, hoping to feel even a slight breeze. As the sun struck her face she could see only sun spots, then reeled and toppled forward into the onions that grew in the burning hot muck.

"Mr. Anderson!" shouted the big girl nearest to Kate.

Ivan looked up quickly. He reached Kate in a few giant leaps. "Bob, get some water!" The long-legged youth standing helplessly by, ran for the pump. Ivan tenderly picked up his wife and carried her to a grassy spot beneath the trees at the edge of the field. He straightened her out, opened her shirt collar and pulled up her sleeves. The girl who had first called Ivan retrieved the hat where it had fallen and started fanning her. When the water arrived, Ivan shook out his blue handkerchief and dabbed the cold water across her temples and all over her face and arms.

Kate was conscious several moments before she dared open her eyes. Finally she said with a weak smile, "Just throw it all on me; I'm back with the living." A small titter went around the group. She would always remember the drawn anxious look on Ivan's face when she first opened her eyes and saw him bending over her. "I guess it's time the city gal minds her husband and takes the rest of the afternoon off."

"The rest of the afternoon and the rest of the week!" Ivan said with determination. "Let's knock off for a drink now, I don't want anymore of you passing out on me."

As Kate walked shakily beside Ivan back to the house, her only thought was that the whole community would be hearing that Ivan Anderson's wife fainted in the onion field.

Kate slept the rest of the afternoon, awakening every so often aware of the heat, then slept again.

The weeders quit short of four o'clock. After Ivan had taken them home he washed and got himself a glass of iced tea and a couple of cookies. Carrying the tea with him, he walked to the bedroom door where Kate now lay awake thinking about the dishes still waiting to be washed.

"Want some?" He held the glass out to her. She took a drink, then lay back down, not knowing quite what to say. He sat on the bed beside her and picked up her hand and looked at it, where the muck had dug under the nails.

"You work out there day after day and I couldn't even take six hours of it."

He replaced her hand, smoothed back the matted hair at her temples, then took a deep breath. "You know I'm not much for making sentimental speeches, but here's one I'm going to try. I should have made it yesterday when you got this idea about weeding onions."

Kate saw the earnest look on his face in spite of the tiredness and wondered what was coming.

"I didn't marry you to get a field hand. Besides being very, very much in love with you, I thought of you as being in my house to come home to, all fresh and clean and pretty like you have been up to today, when I come in tired, dirty and hungry. I know that's not so simple in this muck country and the heat. But don't give in to it, Kate, certainly not with any thought of helping me."

He paused not looking at her directly, but fingering the lace at the top of the slip in which she had been sleeping. "A lot of the women around here do work in the fields and do chores. I suppose some of them got into the habit just recently when everyone was trying desperately to hang on to their farms through the depression. Maybe it saved them, I don't know. But as for me, I can't see where that much is gained. Maybe during a brief emergency like getting in hay before it rains, I might have to ask you to come out and drive the tractor, or to feed the chickens when I have to be gone until late, something like that. But I don't want you ever to have to do heavy, hard outside work like women weren't intended to do." He sighed again and went on, looking intently at her now. "There will be people who don't agree with our way of doing things. It may set us apart from other families. But I don't care, do you?"

Her eyes filled with tears as she slowly moved her head from side to side and her mind flashed back to her conversation with Mrs. Verbank. How desperate she had felt then, wanting to do things a little different. She took his hand and laid it beneath her cheek wet with tears. "It's the way I want us to live, too. You have your work and I have mine. But it looked to me like that arrangement on a farm is too lopsided. I'm not even sure that's what sent me out to weed onions. Maybe it was just because I enjoy a challenge. I wasn't out there an hour before I knew it was a big mistake. Do you honestly feel I'm doing enough with just the housework and garden?"

"Of course I do. Maybe I grew up just taking women's work for granted. Now I'm aware of what gets done – and how hard it's been for you. But for me to come in and find the house all neat and pretty, you the same without a complaint, iced tea waiting in the refrigerator – that's what it takes for a man to rest awhile, then start in again."

"I'm sorry for just one day when you had to come in and find dirty dinner dishes still on the table at five o'clock in the afternoon."

The heart to heart conversation between husband and wife ended in a long close embrace, during which neither was aware of the sweltering heat of the July afternoon surrounding them.

CHAPTER 12

News

THE NEXT MORNING Ivan was up and out to his chores when Kate awakened, even though it was just daylight – and still warm. She was aware of being very, very thirsty. How strange so early in the morning. She got out of bed and went to the kitchen where Ivan nearly always put a fresh pail of water first thing in the morning. She poured a glass full from the dipper and took a long drink. It was no sooner down than she grabbed the wash basin and, hanging over it, tottered back to bed. What could be the matter? Or had she just drunk too fast. She didn't feel otherwise sick. What had they had for supper last night? Was Ivan feeling all right? It would be disastrous for him to get sick now. Maybe she was still feeling the effects of too much sun and heat yesterday. A fine way to start the day when she was determined to be a good housewife who never neglects her duties.

Suddenly, like the wave of nausea that swept over her as she turned on her side, a thought struck her – morning sickness! Could it be, in spite of all their precautions? The dizziness yesterday before she even went out in the sun. She'd fainted and never had before. She'd been so tired and wanting to sleep these last few days. A late period, even irregular as she was. She couldn't be real sure yet – but what if? What would Ivan think about the added expense of it? They had planned to wait awhile.

If she wasn't already up when he came in for the milk pails, he usually came in to waken her. She heard him coming through the house and, smiling wanly, turned her head slowly toward the door.

He took in the covered wash basin beside her and her pale face. "The heat still got you down, huh?"

"I think you better bring me the box of crackers."

"Crackers?" His face was merely puzzled.

"Do you know why women eat crackers in bed? Or why even strong ones faint sometimes?"

Ivan thought for a moment, then frowned. "No, why do they?" Looking worried, he sat down on the bed beside her.

She gulped and closed her eyes as the bed jiggled. "Did you ever hear of morning sickness? Or don't cows have that before they calve?"

For a moment he looked incredulous. "You couldn't be!"

"Well, I am, or pretty sure of it." His change of expression to a grin did not escape Kate's heavy eyes as he bent over her. She pushed him gently away and gulped again. "Oh, don't touch me now. I feel like heaving every time I move. Just get the crackers, even though I don't know how I'll keep any down."

He hurried to the kitchen. Kate heard him knock into a chair and something fall heavily out of the cupboard onto the floor. "How long has this been going on? Are you really sure about it? When will it be?" One question after another tumbled out as he fumbled with the box of crackers.

She was not too sick to be amused at him. She laid a section of crackers at her side, dreading to try it. "I *don't* know for sure yet, but if I can believe what I've read and been told, I've surely got the symptoms. Maybe it will come on our first anniversary or maybe we'll have an Easter lily." She looked closely at his face, trying to discover his real feelings. "Do you mind it's so soon, honey?"

"So soon? That sounds like an awful long time for you to be sick every morning. Can't you speed it up a little?"

"Oh, I won't be sick all the time. Just for awhile, maybe not then if I eat my crackers in time, so they tell me."

Ivan looked at his watch. "Well gosh, I've got to milk yet. Those kids will be waiting on me for sure if I don't hurry. You just stay right there and eat your crackers. I'll get something for breakfast when I get the chores done."

"Not if I can help it. This is part of women's work, you know." He kissed her meekly on the forehead without otherwise touching her and hurried out.

Milking the cows was always a time for thinking and this morning Ivan had plenty to think about. So they were going to have a baby already. He forced thoughts of the added expense to the back of his mind so that he could be excited about it.Would it be a boy or a girl? He supposed every father was eager for a son. But a girl would be fine, too. Whichever it was, it would begin a new generation, the fifth, on this farm. The great, great grandchild of Andrew and Susan Stangland.

If it turned out to be a boy, would he be farming here someday? What if they never had a son? By the time a child grew up, some women might choose farming as a career whether or not they were married. His mother and aunts raised chickens, a few sheep or had little patches of onions to call their own. It was the only way they had to make money for themselves.

Ivan continued his thoughts with his head half buried in a cow's flank, the streams of milk zinging into the empty pail. He'd already hung a full pail on a hook by the wall while he finished milking in the second pail and could take them both to the house at the same time.

The three barn cats happily lapped from the pan on the floor where he'd poured some milk for them. Smiling, he remembered as a boy how he used to relieve the boredom of milking by squirting a tit full of milk at the cats as they stood by meowing for their pan to be filled.

His thinking shifted to another matter. It was time this farm had a name. Strangely it never had had one that he knew of. It had always been referred to as "the home place." Maybe that would be a good name when they finally got around to painting the barn. Other farms had names lettered on their barns. Names like Golden Acres, Fertile Acres, Sunnyside Farm, Meadow View. He'd been visioning a red barn with white letters, but he'd let Kate decide about the house. She'd have some ideas about a name, too.

He unlatched the stanchion holding in the last cow and she backed out to follow the rest of the small herd to the pasture to begin manufacturing for the evening milking.

With a full pail of milk in each hand, Ivan hurried to the house and smelled bacon frying. The sun was just coming up.

CHAPTER 13

Strange Trip To Town

THE ONION WEEDING was finished; the heat continued with little rain or relief. Kate and Ivan were resting after lunch. She was on the couch. He was stretched out on the floor beside her. "Would you like to take the milk check into the bank this afternoon?" he asked.

"If you think you can trust me with all that money."

"I wish I could tell you to spend it any way you want."

"I've got all I want – you and him." She put one hand down on Ivan and patted her mid-section with the other.

When Ivan had gone back to the fields, Kate began washing dishes, sighing as she noticed the black muck which had sifted in all over the house. It was time to reclean the downstairs and she hadn't even started on the upstairs. That part of the house hovered over her and kept beckoning. Not that they needed the rooms, but she was eager to apply her ideas. But that would require refinishing second-hand furniture, and between the heat and her pregnancy, she couldn't tolerate the smell of paint now. Beneath her, at least, in the cool stone cellar, sparkling on a shelf, were canned strawberries, raspberries, cherries and tiny red beet pickles. Now it was time to can peaches. Of all the household kitchen tasks, she enjoyed canning the most. She'd even gone into the County Agriculture Extension office in Richland to get bulletins on the latest methods.

She finished the dishes and hung up the towel. Then she stood momentarily at the window, looking out over the dry, hot, muck fields towards the Rockwells. Some or all of their children went swimming just about every day, usually in the evening after their chores were done. Kate smiled, remembering the evening last week when the three girls came past the house, dresses over their bathing suits. Clara and Mary were carrying on a lively chatter; Michelle walked silently alongside. When she saw Kate and Ivan on the front porch, she said to her sisters, "I'm going to stop here. I'll meet you on the way back."

Shelly told Kate and Ivan that the last time they went swimming she got a "yucky" old leech on her and she wasn't anxious to go again. She'd rather cool off in a wash tub of water out in the yard, she said. At least it was clean. Ivan enjoyed the little neighbor he'd seen grow up, and kidded with her and matched wits. She often came up with something very wise or funny, making them laugh or marvel at her scope of comprehension.

Kate moved her attention to Mattie Enders' little house. How would she be taking the hot weather and what would she be doing? Probably sweltering in those dark warm clothes. Kate hadn't talked to her since the day she'd stopped for a start of the little Bleeding Heart flowers which Mattie had offered her.

An idea struck her. On impulse again she reached for the telephone and rang a short and a long, a signal seldom heard on the busy party line. A gruff, weary-sounding voice answered. "Mrs. Enders, this is Kate Anderson. I have to go into town alone this afternoon and I thought maybe you'd ride along."

"I ain't got nothin' to git in town t'day." There was a pause during which Kate could hear heavy breathing. "Miz Rockwell usually takes me when I need to go in for something."

"Oh, go along anyway. The ride will do us both good. I'm not going to be there long. I just have to get to the bank before it closes at three o'clock and get some groceries."

There was a longer pause this time. "Well, stop out front as you go by. I'll be see'in 'bout it."

At two-thirty when Kate pulled up in front of the Enders' place, she wondered: Would Mattie be ready to go, ignore her or chase her away? Whatever it was, she hoped it wouldn't take long or she'd be late for the bank. The heavy curtains at the front window parted ever so slightly, then a moment later Mattie came out the door, closed and locked it behind her and hobbled spryly toward the car. She was obviously dressed up in a shiny silk dress with long sleeves and a well-worn old-fashioned black straw hat with a narrow rim and a bunch of purple flowers at the front. An old black oilcloth handbag swung at her side. She looked so warm. Poor old soul.

Kate reached across the front seat and opened the door. Before she had a chance to speak, Mattie remarked bluntly, "You ain't got much time to make it to the bank." She pulled herself up onto the seat, tucked in her skirt and after a couple of attempts got the door closed after her. Kate waited until

Mattie was firmly settled before she put the car into gear and drove on. Mattie held tightly to the opened window at her side. Few words passed between them. There wasn't much Kate could think of to say without including Ivan. She parked the car in the shade along the courthouse square.

Again Mattie spoke before Kate had a chance. "You hurry along to the bank now. I'll wait right here in the shade. Like I said, I ain't got nothin' to git."

Kate deposited the check at the bank, went to the ten-cent store to pick up a couple of items and stopped at the Kroger store to get her groceries. The clerks all knew her now and called her Mrs. Anderson. One of them carried the two sacks across the street and deposited them in the back seat. Then Kate spoke eagerly to the old lady still sitting in the same position as when she'd left her. "Let's go across the street and have some ice cream before we go home."

"Go along an' do whatever you want. I'll still be here when you git back."

"Oh, I wouldn't go alone. I'd feel silly sitting in there eating ice cream all by myself."

Mattie glanced at the streets outside, then down at her dress as though trying to think of a good excuse. "I ain't dressed jest right or nothin', it's been so long since I been in a ice cream store."

"Come on," Kate urged and opened the door for her, "You look just fine."

"Well, I'll go along, but don't know as I want nothin'. Mebby a cup o' tea." She hesitatingly climbed out, looked furtively up and down the sidewalk, then stood awkwardly beside her companion in the short sleeved summer dress. They slowly crossed the street to the popular Sweet Shop.

Kate led the way into the ice cream parlor cooled by an overhead fan, then to an inconspicuous table in a near corner where they settled themselves on the round-bottomed wire-backed chairs and drew themselves up to the round table. There were only two other customers at that time of day. The waitress from behind the counter came across the black and white checked floor to serve them.

"I want a peach sundae," said Kate. "Wouldn't you like one too, Mrs. Enders?"

"Just bring me a dish o' vanilly ice cream," said the old lady, glancing around as though she was afraid of being heard.

"Are you sure you wouldn't like some peaches on it? Ivan and I had one Saturday night and they're very good."

"Put some sauce on it if you want," Mattie finally agreed.

Kate nodded to the waitress. The girl smiled and went back behind the counter. In a few minutes she returned with two long dishes each containing a large scoop of ice cream covered with sweet juicy slices of fresh peaches. The sundaes were even larger, Kate noticed, than those she and Ivan had had.

Kate eagerly began eating the sundae, knowing she would not be hungry for supper, but she was glad to be enjoying it with Mattie. What conversation there was Kate had to carry. She talked about her flowers, her garden and the things she'd canned, the first she'd ever done alone. And wasn't it nice and cool in here?

The old lady kept her eyes down as though concentrating only on the food before her. She did comment that she and Robert, her son, used to get ice cream at the old drugstore once in awhile, but it wasn't there anymore.

When both had finished, Kate again led the way out, stopping first to pay at the counter. Mattie dug into her oilcloth bag. "No," Kate said, "this is my treat. Maybe the next time we come, I'll let you treat me."

Back in the car and headed home, Kate said, "I haven't had much appetite lately, but that sundae tasted good. You see, Mrs. Enders, we're expecting a baby and I get kind of weak-kneed sometimes. I guess that's one reason I asked you to come along today. I feel a little better when someone is with me."

Mattie sat rigidly in her seat. "Afraid I wouldn't be much help 'bout the drivin' o' a machine if you git one o' yer weak spells."

"Oh, I'm all right, really, it's just comforting to have someone along. Ivan needs to be in the fields. The Rockwells are so good to us, I can always depend on them, but they are forever busy, too."

As they neared Mattie's place, Kate continued, "I do so miss my mother. We did so many things together. I never knew either of my grandmothers. They both died before I was old enough to remember."

Mattie fidgeted around on the seat, then took a deep shaky breath before she burst out, "Ain't yer man told you nothin' 'bout me yet? Or the Rockwells or anybody?"

"Mrs. Enders, I haven't even told Ivan we've met. I thought maybe someday you'd tell me all you wanted me to know. Then we could forget it and *we* could be neighbors even if you don't like *him*."

"Oh, I ain't got nothin' 'gainst him, I guess. Was his pa thet didn't do right by me." They had driven up in front of the house, but Mattie made no move to get out, so Kate turned off the motor and sat ready to listen.

"First off I ain't Mrs. Enders, I never been married." Kate's mind flashed immediately to the son, Robert . . . Ivan's father? . . . no, that couldn't be. "When Robert was 10, I brought him up here from Kentucky, folks down there said he could earn his own way weedin' onions and such. We settled on this here place and it was a purty good life. He was a weedin' onions to beat the band and doin' chores fer people, proud to bring thet money home. Finally it got so we could even farm on our own, didn't need any outsiders to pay. We went to church most Sundays," her breath caught in a dry sob, "and when they found out I could play the pie-anna, I substituted fer the regular pie-anna player."

Kate waited for the bubble to burst as Mattie hurried on with her story, the words tumbling out as though if she stopped she couldn't start again. Her voice was high and thin. "We was busy farmin,' Robert an' me, but sometimes, like you, I'd have to go into town. Only then it was with horse an' buggy an' took most o' the day." Mattie struggled for control again. "Then when Robert got into thet trouble . . . went to Art fer help . . . too late, Robert was already dead . . . next thing Art an' another high-and-mighty from the church came here a-telling' me I can't have the funeral in the church. Well, I drove 'em off with Robert's 22 an' told 'em to never speak to me again or expect me to play their ol' pie-anna."

"Oh, Mattie, Mattie!" Kate reached over and gripped the bony arm in the black long sleeve.

But Mattie Enders opened the car door, slid out and went bowed and weeping toward her door. When Kate saw she was safely inside, she sat for a moment wondering if she should follow her in, decided against it and shakily drove on home.

So the trouble had something to do with the church. That hadn't occurred to her. Now she was ready to tell Ivan what she knew about Mattie and let him fill in the missing links. What kind of trouble was Robert in that he got killed or died or something? How could it be so bad that his funeral couldn't be held in the church? What kind of Christianity was that? So it was Mattie herself playing the piano she had heard as she went by one day.

Kate waited till after supper, when they were lingering over coffee, before she nervously took up the subject with Ivan. "Honey, I've been keeping a secret from you."

"Don't tell me we're going to have twins."

"No," she laughed, "nothing like that. I have become quite good friends with Mattie Enders."

"What!" he shouted and frowned. "Has she been down here bothering you?"

"No, no, no," Kate calmed him. "Remember the day I asked who lived in the little house with the pretty flowers? That was the day I first met her. I saw her working in the garden and I just stopped to say hello."

"Oh, Kate, you shouldn't have," Ivan spoke with alarm.

"Ivan, she is just a really lonesome bitter old soul. At my request, she came down and spent an hour or so one afternoon when you were gone, going over the flowers with me, telling me what they were and giving advice."

"You've got to be kidding!"

"No, really. And would you believe she went with me to Richland today, and waited in the car till I got through shopping? Then I persuaded her to go with me to have peach sundaes at the Sweet Shop."

Ivan shook his head. "I must be dreaming. You and Mattie Enders in the Sweet Shop! Does she know who you are?"

"Of course, and furthermore she said she 'guessed' she didn't have anything against you, 'just your pa.' Then she tried to tell me all about the trouble, or all that she was willing for me to know, but ended up crying till she couldn't finish. By then we were parked in front of her house, so she just broke off and went inside."

"It sounds like you know as much or more about it than I do." Relief was evident in his voice. "It was such a hush-up subject around our house and the church. It was something you just didn't ask questions about."

"Just because he was illegitimate? That doesn't seem like enough reason for the church to refuse his funeral, even that long ago."

"I think he stole a horse or committed some kind of crime."

"Mattie said there was trouble and she came to your dad about it."

"*Came* to Dad?"

"Yes. Then she said something about it being too late. Robert was dead and they wouldn't let her hold the funeral in the church."

"Hm-m, that is strange. I was only nine or ten when it happened. Claud was probably 11 and Helga 13. My memory of it is pretty sketchy. I just remember being suddenly cut off from ever again going to Aunt Mattie Enders' place. And she never came here after the conversation we overheard one night on the front porch."

"What was that?"

"It was a Sunday afternoon and the three of us had just come back from swimming in the lake. It was dusk. We were never supposed to stay back there after it started getting dark. The lamp in the kitchen hadn't been lighted yet, so they didn't see us come in. But we could see Dad out on the front wall with his head in his hands. He was saying, 'That poor woman, that poor woman, what can we do?' Mom was out there, too, and old Amos Walls with his long, white beard, along with some other man. As I remember, one of them said, 'We can't have the funeral in our church. Reverend Medler just won't accept it. He says he's even against her playing the piano and flaunting that fatherless boy in front of our young people.' Then Dad said, 'I was trying to tell her some of us would come out to her house and the cemetery to give him a Christian burial.' That's all we heard because Helga said we had to get on upstairs and get dressed. Claud said he heard the next day that Mattie chased Dad and the other fellows off with a gun."

"Heavens. I wonder what kind of trouble he was in. Do you suppose he was killed?"

"I wonder. It seems like Robert was gone for weeks before that. We imagined he was in a hospital or sanitarium or something, like another neighbor we knew. We never suspected he was in prison – if that's where he was. We felt bad, because we liked Robert. He took us rabbit and squirrel hunting and told great tales about the Kentucky horse farm where he and his mother used to live. When I was older I realized they were just tall tales. He didn't use that hillbilly language, though, like his mother."

"Did Robert seem to be retarded?"

"Oh, no, he wasn't dumb at all. He told me about the stars and constellations, using big words I couldn't understand. I always remember a fact he taught me about arithmetic when I was learning multiplication tables. He asked me if I knew what 9 times 99 was. Of course I didn't. He said. 'That's easy, just take 100 times 9, that's 900 and take off the 9 and you get 991.' I remembered that and used it over and over."

"What did he look like?"

"He was nice looking, at least I thought he was. Not very big, light curly hair. I couldn't understand why people looked down on him, until I learned what illegitimate meant."

"What was Mattie like then?"

"She always seemed like a nice lady. She was not a big woman, solemn, dark hair. But what I remember most were her gingerbread and sorghum molasses cookies. Robert would bring us out some or sometimes she'd invite us all in for gingerbread and cocoa. But later she was just a bitter old recluse who didn't go anywhere or have any company."

"Poor old dear." Kate was obviously moved. "She said Mrs. Rockwell takes her into town when she needs to go."

"Yes. I think they look out for her and take things to her. Rockwells bought their farm and moved here awhile after Robert died. Clara and Mary were just little then. I imagine Dad urged them to befriend her since he couldn't."

"Your Mother and Mattie were such good friends," Kate said sadly. "I could tell that from what she said and how she knew all about the flowers down here."

Ivan said nothing more for quite awhile as they both thought about the situation. Ivan recognized a new dimension in Kate. She had come into this community and in less than six months solved a neighborhood problem of 15 years standing. What else did she have up that sleeve besides an arm, which he now lovingly caressed.

As Kate washed the dishes, the loose ends to the story kept haunting her. Surely someday she'd hear enough more from Mattie to fit the pieces together if she didn't pry. She hoped Mattie was all right after the emotional upheaval of the afternoon. Tomorrow she'd think of some excuse to call her. Maybe there would be a time she could visit with her in private again and tell her how crushed Arthur Anderson had been when he had to let her down. Who on earth was the minister at that time to have so little compassion for a sorrowing mother at the loss of her only child? She hadn't asked Ivan about him.

CHAPTER 14

Farmers Only

MAYBE IT WAS A LETTER from her brother, Tommy, which came in the morning's mail. Maybe it was the prospects of another week of humid heat. Or maybe it was the accumulation of several things that added up to depression that Kate couldn't shake off on a day in late August.

Ivan hadn't even read the letter from Tommy that noon though she offered it to him first thing. And when she'd tried to tell him about it at the dinner table, he mumbled an absent, "Is that so?" and "When is that to be?" Then he went back into another silence and she knew it was because the onion tops were turning prematurely yellow from too much heat and dry weather. The corn, too, was suffering, their long broad leaves curling up into ropes. After dinner he'd read the paper for a few minutes, then went back to work without a cheerful or a loving word.

She lay on the floor with her pillow near the north door, trying to catch any bit of breeze. But there was none stirring; no relief here.

Probably she should have dropped the subject of Tommy's approaching marriage and encouraged Ivan to talk about the crops when she could see he wasn't interested in anything else. Onions! Onions! Onions! Everything here revolves around a stupid onion. They're our bread and butter, our clothes, our home – everything! And they depend on the weather. Earning a living on a farm shouldn't be like this. Wouldn't there ever be a time when they could live a more carefree life – go out more often, see more people their own age and talk about something besides crops, the weather and farm chores? Ivan kept telling her the fall and winter would be different, but if the crops were turning out as bad as he seemed to think, how could it be better – with no money?

Her thoughts again turned to Oregon and – home. Today, for instance, her father might come home from the office early and suggest they drive up to the mountain cabin for the weekend. They'd convince Mother . . .

No, no, no! She must not think about it. She threw the pillow back onto the bed, went to the kitchen, took down the fly swatter and began swatting flies. They were all over the house again. Now there were these little gnats called oat bugs, so tiny they come right through the screens and could hardly be seen until you felt them crawling on you. They seemed to be a new pest in the community. Serena Rockwell said they would leave when the oats was cut.

She'd try to figure out this riddle about Tommy. Maybe that would make the afternoon go faster. Why in the world had he taken up with May Bell White? And getting married so soon. His last letter sounded a little like he was looking, but, oh, Tommy, not May Bell! He wrote that she had gone to secretarial school following graduation from high school the year after Tommy, the year before Kate. Now she was secretary to a new law firm in town, Tommy said, and would be quitting soon because she wanted to be a "full-time wife." Was that anything to be suspicious of? Perhaps she'd changed since they, the girls in high school, used to secretly refer to her as "Lily White" always playing up to teachers and other adults of authority. She was blond, good-looking, nice figure, lots of dates, but never a steady that Kate was aware of. The boys soon tired of her self-centeredness. Now . . . poor gullible Tommy. Should she write and warn him just in case May Bell hadn't changed?

No, she must not do that. If they went ahead and married anyway, it would strain the relationship between them, and anything would be better than that. Of course they couldn't go to the wedding. Ivan would urge her to go. But even if they could afford it, it would be no fun without her husband. She'd probably end up using some of the money she had left for a nice wedding gift for them. There was too little to do what she wanted with the upstairs anyway. She listlessly hung up the fly swatter, put on her garden hat and went outdoors. Maybe a walk to the woods would help her mood.

She was dripping with perspiration by the time she reached the shade from the trees in the woods. In a far field she could see Ivan on the tractor pulling the hay rake. She found the coolest looking spot and sat down to fan herself with her hat. But it was not cool. The grass was crisp and dry and the oat bugs found her. With a sigh she rose and walked on toward the lake by crossing the corner of an onion field, the muck burning her legs as it dusted up in front and behind her. She sought out the place where they had had the pleasant little picnic that day in June. There was hardly any resemblance now. The weeds had hidden the grass and were almost knee high. The water around part of the lake's edge was mossy, even scummy, as Ivan said it would be.

She walked over to the wooden-plank bridge which connected the onion field on one side of the ditch with the silo-corn, as Ivan called it, on the other side. An elm tree at the corner shaded the hot afternoon sun from the bridge. Kate sat down at the edge of the rough wooden boards and hung her feet over the edge. Besides melting drop by drop, she was very, very tired. Why had she come back here on such a day? It was a long walk home. Her eyes followed the ditch as far as she could see until it curved out of sight. The bank was overgrown with unsightly weeds and nettles. The ditch water, like the lake's edge, was green.

All the streams here seemed to be sluggish, usually muddy, not tumbling and crystal-clear as they were in the West. Memories of that far away place overtook her: her father coming home early from the office to suggest going; persuading her mother to drop whatever she was doing, whatever plans she'd made; getting a few supplies together; and after an hour's drive, the cool-mountain-forest, the lodge with the clean, cold creek running by, and she and Tommy playing in it. Great shaking sobs overtook her as she cried loud and long. Never before had she felt this terrible homesickness. Not in the two weeks away from home at camp for the first time when she was ten years old, or winters at college. Even girls who lived in the same state got homesick, but not Kate. She was too busy and having too much fun. Now here she was happily married to a good man and a mother-to-be and wretchedly homesick. She missed her father and mother and brother as much as any child. How long would this horrible feeling last? Why didn't she admit to herself – if not to Ivan – that she hated this farm, this country life? But what good would it do if she did?

Gradually the sobs then the tears subsided. She felt the first bit of relief she'd felt all day when this depression settled over her. She noticed the heat no less, but the inside heavy feeling had lifted. She felt like walking back home now; there would be supper to start soon. A sudden thought struck her: There would be one spot reasonably cool. She smiled to herself and started planning. Maybe it would help bring Ivan out of some of his depression, too.

They usually ate supper before Ivan milked, deciding it was the logical thing to do since he had to come in for the milk things and to wash first anyway. Also, Kate could wash the dishes while he was milking and they would both be through about the same time.

About five-thirty Ivan came slowly towards the house, not even hungry on such a day – just hot, sticky and discouraged. If they were working in Chicago now, he would take a refreshing shower and they'd go out to an air-conditioned restaurant for supper and maybe a movie, if they could afford it. At least they'd have a pay check and know how much they had and for how long it had to last. What was the use to think about it? He'd made the decision. Too late now to change his mind, at least until he'd given it a fair trial. He even dreaded going in to face Kate, the mood he was in.

She was on the back porch noisily chipping ice and dropping it into the pitcher of whatever it was, something pink. She had on a lime-green organdy dress, her legs bare except for a coat of tan that extended down to the red-polished toes showing out of white sandals.

"Am I supposed to come in or stay out? You must be having company." She didn't look as though she'd shed a drop of perspiration all day.

"Come in, silly. You're the best and only company I have. But be sure and wash behind your ears, because we're going out to supper this evening."

"Going out?" he asked crossly.

"Don't worry, darling, we're not going far."

"The devil with a picnic this evening," he muttered. He glanced around the kitchen. There was no evidence of prepared food. Not even the picnic basket. If they were going to the Rockwells' she wouldn't be making the punch. He went to the wash stand and washed his hands, then splashed the cool water over his face and neck, not caring for once how far away the splatters landed.

Kate held out a clean blue shirt. "Put this on. It will make you feel a little better."

"Over all this sweat and dirt?" He was more irritated than she anticipated.

"You'll feel a little fresher." He grudgingly removed the soggy shirt, threw it towards the corner of the porch and put on the clean one. "Now follow me."

She led the way to the narrow door at the corner of the porch and started carefully down the stairs to the cellar, the hem of her wide skirt brushing the well-scrubbed steps behind her and in front of him. Then he noticed the sign hanging overhead at the bottom of the steps:

YE OLDE CELLAR
C-O-O-L
(Farmers only Admitted)

For the first time all day he was amused enough to smile. The cool gray-dark settled over him. The meal was neatly laid out on a red-checked tablecloth spread over the wobble-legged table that always sat down there. The only light came through the small window at ground level. Ivan lifted his wife's chin and kissed her, the icy pitcher between them.

They sat on the kitchen chairs, which Kate had previously brought down, and leisurely began the meal. In this familiar yet strange cool room, part of the day's heat and discouragement started dropping from Ivan and he ate heartily.

Kate didn't eat much, but was enjoying the meal in one of her favorite spots of the whole house. Ivan hadn't taken her here on their first pilgrimage through the house that day back in March when she first arrived. She had discovered the cellar all by herself the next day. It was just the single room, not large, but it reminded Kate of butter churns and sweet-smelling cream, homemade jellies and pickles which had surely, in their time, been kept there. Overhead were the heavy beams from the kitchen floor; the sides were field stone like the house foundation and the wall along the front porch. Along one side and one end were wooden racks filled with fruit jars, some full, some empty and turned upside down. The floor was rough cement. On further back was the dugout from the old house. Kate had curtained it off.

"Don't you wonder why I've kept this part of the house so clean?"

"You have been doing an excellent job of housekeeping all the way around, my dear. I've been thinking of keeping you on."

"All the time, except for one day," Kate laughed.

They finished their meal along with lots of small talk. The chilled chocolate pudding with cream to top it was a good ending to the supper, but they lingered on in the cool quiet of the underground room. There were no flies here, no oat bugs.

Ivan reached across the small table and took his wife's sunbrowned hands in his darker, rough ones. He looked at her with devotion. "Precious Kate, not a complaint or a word about being out here in this gosh-awful heat. Even the old-timers say it's been one of the hottest summers they remember. And it had to be your first."

Kate kept her eyes down, not looking at him, as memories of the afternoon battle with herself raced back to her. She was thankful that she'd fought it out alone and not carried it to Ivan.

"Isn't that what you told me I was supposed to be?" she teased, composure regained, "the lazy little wife all dressed up to meet her tired, hungry husband?"

"Not even an old slave-driver like me could expect it today," he grinned back.

"You'll get over your fancy ideas someday. But I hope not." She gave his hands an extra squeeze.

"All I need now, besides rain, is some way to take a shower. I've been thinking how to make one, running water and all."

"Tell me quick."

"You know those big pails with the spigot at the bottom? We used to sell them at the implement store in Chicago. Well, I'm going to buy one, fill it with water and hang it on a hook in the corner of the woodshed – there where the foundation is broken out – turn on the spigot to just the right drizzle, take a shower and let the water run outside."

Kate laughed merrily. "I suppose it would work. I might even use it myself."

"And let one of the neighbors catch you?"

"How about you? If one of the Rockwell women – or worse yet, Mattie Enders . . . She'd really fry your wicked name in oil!"

Laughing and lingering over the last of the fruit punch, neither of them wanting to go back upstairs, Ivan said, "Let's take that trip to Lake Michigan this weekend, forget the crops and the farm, find someplace we can relax for a couple of days."

"Oh, honey, let's do."

"We'll be reckless for once and worry about the expense when we get back."

"Sure! We can live on beans and . . . and green onions for the next two weeks if we have to."

"*Yellow* green onions, you mean. And we can teach the pigs and chickens to eat saw dust." He leaned back and put his hands behind his head. "Tell me now about Tommy. He's getting married you say?"

CHAPTER 15

The Thunderstorm

THEIR WEEKEND IN CHICAGO was one to be remembered. Without going overboard they ate in air-conditioned restaurants, showered in tile-lined bathrooms and swam in the surf of Lake Michigan.

Then it was back to the farm and the chores which a neighbor, Bill Bryce, had done for Ivan in their absence.

Monday morning following Kate and Ivan's weekend off was as hot as before. But the weather forecast was finally news – and cause for rejoicing. The battery-operated radio predicted thunder showers by evening.

Immediately upon hearing the report, Earnie Rockwell came down to where Ivan was hoeing Canada thistles and asked him to help get in the rest of his hay before the rain came. Ivan readily agreed. "It'll be a dilly, too, after all this heat," Rocky called back as he hurried up the lane to rig the wagon with the hay rack.

"I know they won't hear of me coming home for dinner," Ivan told Kate a few minutes later. "Better come on up at noon."

Kate thought longingly for a moment. There was a standing invitation to come to the Rockwells anytime. "No, I think I better not. The rain might come suddenly and I've got clothes on the line and windows are open all over the house. I don't want to close them until I know for sure it's going to rain."

"Well, let's hope it does. He hasn't got much hay this cutting, so we should be done by early afternoon. Then I'll be home and we can celebrate the rain together."

Kate kissed him goodbye and watched out the window as he walked toward the Rockwells. She didn't like thunderstorms and hoped he'd be home. Thankfully, there would be no dinner to get except a sandwich for herself.

By one o'clock hot sunshine still prevailed without a rain cloud in sight. The air was motionless. Inky-black wash water from the muck and perspiration-soaked clothes waited Ivan's return to be emptied. Kate had her sandwich with a glass of milk and was more than ready to rest. In spite of the heat, she knew she would sleep.

It was after two when she awakened, covered with perspiration and oat bugs. She got up, groggy and nauseated, nibbled crackers and felt better. Looking outside, she found there actually were clouds gathering in the sky to the north and west. She wondered how the haying was going or if they were already done. She'd seen the loads coming in until they stopped for noon. She hoped Ivan would come soon. Already she was beginning to worry about the storm. They'd had a couple of thunderstorms before the big heat wave started and Ivan laughed at her uneasiness. "Wait till a really good one comes along." This might be it.

She took down and neatly folded the things from the line that were dry, noticing the bright streaks of lightning that now flashed across the darkening sky. She'd leave the rest of the clothes on the line as long as possible. Maybe they would finish drying before the rain came. She looked again to see if Ivan was coming. But no, there was another load of hay just going in. Maybe it was the last.

The sky grew darker and darker as though night were coming on at three in the afternoon. The lightning seemed nearer and more frequent. Small fits of wind sent clouds of dust and muck scurrying, much of it into the house. But she was still reluctant to close the windows. Every moving breath of air, even dust lade, was too precious to shut out.

She tried to busy herself about the kitchen, dampening clothes to iron and thinking about supper. But her mind was taken with the approaching storm and Ivan's return. It was getting so dark she could hardly see without lighting a lamp. She went out the back door and walked toward the barn, wondering if there were anything she should see to. Being alone she felt responsible for the whole farm. The barn and other buildings which had always seemed so friendly now seemed only too quiet and foreboding. The tractor with its high, cleated-steel wheels just below Ivan's small crop of hay already in the mow, resembled a huge monster ready to stir and come to life in the semi-darkness. She shivered and hurried away, her imagination working overtime.

On the way back past the chicken house, she noticed that the chickens were all inside and on the roost as though it were night, so she decided to close and latch that door. Lucky chickens, comfortably settled together while she was all alone. Then she noticed the coop with half-a-dozen hens which Ivan had penned up at the end of the chicken house, to break them from setting and to start them laying again, he'd said. She didn't understand why and didn't ask. They, too, had settled down, but with their bills apart and panting. Their water pan had been upset. She should have come out at noon and checked them, as Ivan always did. After watering them, she pulled the piece of old plywood that shaded the side of the coop over the top as far as it would cover and went on to the house. The air now was cooling and she noticed the first raindrops pelting into the inch-thick dust around the chicken house. She wanted to raise her arms to the fresh air and drops of water, the first in so long a time.

The rest of the clothes would have to come down now, dry or not. She hurried, stuffing clothespins into both apron pockets. Already she'd waited too long. The rain was coming faster, the breeze was turning to a wind that nearly whipped the clothes out of her grasp. There were windows all over the house to close yet. She threw the clothes on the kitchen table, dumped out the clothespins, letting them fall where they might and dashed upstairs. The catches on the windows had stuck from remaining in position so long. She had to bump and jar each one until her arms were lame. Great sheets of water came down now. The thunder, proclaimed but briefly by the lightning, boomed loudly overhead. The old trees in the orchard were swaying and bending at the mercy of the wind and rain.

When Kate finally finished upstairs she started down and heard a loud bang, followed by the shatter of breaking glass. It would be that door in the living room blown shut and breaking the glass. She paused momentarily wanting to remain in the windowless stairway, but forced herself to go on down. Why, oh, why hadn't she started closing the house sooner? And where was Ivan!?! She dared not be irritated. He was probably stranded out in the middle of this – maybe even in great danger.

It was raining in everywhere. She could do nothing about the broken glass now. She went from room to room, closing the windows, flinching with each flash of lightning. Now it blazed simultaneously with the crashes of thunder. Each time she felt the next would surely strike the house. Never in her life had she felt so alone, helpless and frightened. Still no Ivan. The wind, whipping up from the cellar window she supposed, was lifting up the kitchen linoleum. She'd have to go down there, too, but she must do something about the broken glass first. The rain was driving in all across the room.

She looked for tacks in the kitchen cabinet drawer, found them, snatched up an old rag rug from the porch and the stone she had been using to hold pickles in brine. Then, with broken glass crunching under her feet, she attempted to tack the rug on the broken window. It took all her strength. Just as she got the last corner battened down, she saw a blinding flash through the east window and heard an electrifying snap along with a terrific crash of thunder. She was paralyzed. The lightning had struck somewhere close. Finally daring to move, she took a quick look out the window. The sturdy old apple tree at the back of the orchard had been split through the middle. It lay there gaping and white with its giant wound.

"Ivan! Ivan!" she screamed. With her last bit of strength, she ran to the cellar, boosted the small window into place, turned the wooden knobs to hold it there, then sank, helpless and defeated by the forces around her, into the chair that had been left there after their pleasant little supper. Here she felt a little apart from the storm, but miles from any other human being.

After what seemed like a long time she heard Ivan's step on the front porch. Almost too weak to move, she lifted her head from her arms and struggled upstairs to where Ivan was shaking the rain from himself and removing Earnie Rockwell's jacket. She threw herself on him. "I was never so frightened in my life," she cried. "The lightning struck a tree in the orchard. It will surely strike the house next!"

"It can't strike the house, honey, or any of the buildings; they all have ground wires." He walked her calmly into the house. "I should have come right home. I had no idea you'd be so frightened."

Kate stiffened and drew back. "Should have come right home!?! Where in heaven's name were you? I supposed you were out in the middle of the hay-field through all this."

"We had the hay in an hour ago." He realized how it must sound to her now. "But you know the Rockwells; the women had ice cream all made and would have been insulted if Bill and I didn't stay for a dish of it."

"An hour to eat a dish of ice cream?" She was seething with fury now instead of fright.

"I'm really sorry. I guess we were so glad for the rain and talking so much, we didn't realize the storm was so bad. Believe me, when I heard that crash down here, I came as fast as I could."

Another ten minutes and the angry storm began to subside. With no indication from Kate that she had forgiven him, Ivan went to change into dry clothes, carefully bringing the wet ones to the back porch and hanging them on a hook. He got a broom and began sweeping up the broken glass, noting with anything but humor, Kate's awkward attempt to cover the broken pane with a rug. He dumped the glass in the now unused coal pail on the porch and went about emptying the wash water. When he returned to the kitchen, Kate was standing with her back to him, looking out the window. It seemed hours since she'd spoken.

"Look how happy the birds are splashing in the puddles."

He walked to her side. Bright daylight had returned. The trees were gently dripping, finally washed free of their coat of dust. "Things never look better than after a big rain when it's been hot and dry so long. Or maybe it's just the sudden contrast."

"Well, I guess it's time to open all those windows I had such a wicked time shutting. I had no idea it would come so sudden or so furious. It's a good thing I don't believe in old wives' tales or this baby would be marked for sure."

Ivan looked at his wife again with unspoken apology, but further words seemed out of place now. "You shut the windows; I'll open them."

Kate went through the kitchen door to the porch and sat in the swing. The air was delightfully cool and fresh smelling. "Is the rain too late to help the onions?" she asked, as Ivan came to join her.

"It won't help the onions, but it will the other crops."

"Where are the oat bugs?"

"The rain probably finished them, along with a lot of other headaches. I doubt if we will have any more really hot weather now, at least at night. I think fall is just around the corner, and I hope it will be pleasant enough to make up to you for all this wretched heat we've had this summer."

"I haven't suffered alone, you know."

They sat in silence enjoying the cool. Then Ivan suddenly laughed. "Did I ever tell you about Grandma Stangland and the fence posts?"

"No. Tell me."

"When they were first married, probably their first summer like ours, Grandpa Tallock spent a long time cutting logs and splitting them into fence posts. He also set a brush pile to burning and thought it was all right to leave when he started off one morning to teach school. Before he left, he asked Grandma to check on the fire once in awhile, because he didn't want it to get over into his fence posts.

"Well, that morning a neighbor lady came by in her buggy and asked Grandma to go fishing with her. She'd brought a lunch and they'd be back before Tallock got home. Grandma loved to fish, so she checked the fire again and it seemed to be all right. She dug some worms, got her fish pole and they took off for Big Lake, which is quite a bit farther away than our little lake. In the meantime, the wind came up and when the women got back home . . ."

"The fence posts were on fire."

"Right. The wind had whipped burning brush into the pile of fence posts and they were blazing so much they couldn't do anything about it."

"I'll bet he was as mad as I was. I can see it runs in the family."

"What, cutting fence posts or teaching school?"

Kate shoved him with her shoulder, making the swing zig zag sideways. "Fishing and eating ice cream when you're supposed to be home!"

Ivan rose laughing. "Well, those cows aren't going to milk themselves. Anyway, it will be cooler in the barn tonight."

"By the way, I shut the chicken house door before the storm. You better let them out. I also covered up the hens in the coop the best I could, but maybe they're all drowned by now."

"Good girl!" he said sincerely, tipped her chin and kissed her.

Kate rose and went into the kitchen where she began picking up the clothespins to return them to the bag hanging on the back porch. Then she folded the clothes dumped on the table and put them in the clothes basket. She could hear Ivan whistling "Ain't Gonna Rain No More" all the way to the barn. "Dopey husbands," she murmered to herself.

CHAPTER 16

Mattie's Piano

IT HAD BEEN A COUPLE OF WEEKS since Mattie's emotional revelation to Kate on the way back from Richland. In spite of the events which had taken place since then, Kate frequently wondered about her neighbor. The day following that trip to town Kate had called and asked, "How are you this morning?"

"Same's always," was the brusque reply, but she'd added with an edge of concern, "You all right?"

"Oh, I'm fine today. I just wanted to tell you that the gladioli bulbs you gave me are starting to bloom. I brought in a red one to go on my marble-top table."

"They finally bloomed, did they?" Then Kate thought she heard the click of a receiver going up – someone listening in – so she quickly ended the brief conversation.

Today was a beautiful late summer day, almost cool. From the porch swing Kate could see the gladioli now, along the fence in a colorful and stately parade. She felt a sudden urge to see the old neighbor again – the person who'd been responsible for a good start on what Kate hoped would eventually be an orderly profusion of flowers.

Ivan would be topping onions in the field all afternoon. She'd walk through the hay field toward Mattie's house. Perhaps she'd invite her in. If not, it would be a pleasant outing anyway. Kate no longer felt any fear, but neither did she want to thrust herself on Mattie.

Kate walked slowly across the field, occasionally stopping to pick a purple clover blossom. After returning from Chicago and the cool weather started, she had papered one of the rooms upstairs with paper she bought at the decorating store where she had formerly worked. She went through the half-price bin and found a purple-pink clover pattern which she promptly fell in love with and there was enough of it to do the room.

The upstairs had delighted her from that first day. The rooms were arranged so nicely, which was unusual in an old house. There was a door to the left, a door to the right and one straight ahead from the stair landing at the top. Each side bedroom had a charmingly sloped ceiling and a dormer window. The third bedroom had the stovepipe from the living room heater going through it, making it warm in winter. She had used the clover-patterned paper in that room and looked back now at the window which overlooked the hay field. Just as I intended, Kate thought.

But with sadness she remembered a small discovery she'd made while cleaning out that room. A box tied with a ribbon was tucked far back on a closet shelf. She supposed it was more old letters which she was always interested in, but on an impulse opened it out of curiosity. Inside was a little old-fashioned doll, well worn as though it had been much loved. Under it was a little pair of black button shoes, still encrusted with mud around the soles. Kate carefully lifted them out of the box and beneath were two little cards with fancy scrolls. On one was printed Alice Lenora Stangland. On the other was Bela William Stangland. That would be Ivan's grandma and grandpa's first two children who died from the flux epidemic. Tears came to her eyes as she fondled the precious possessions put away so many years ago by a mother in abject sorrow. Kate decided to urge Ivan to give them to Helga. She would remember her grandmother even better than Ivan.

She neared the Enders' cluster of buildings: house, wood shed, outhouse and a very dilapidated small barn. She could see Mattie pumping a pail of water. The old lady left the pail hooked over the spout of the pump and straightened up with difficulty. "I thought thet was you a comin' crost the field. Jest gittin' some water to start a boiling fer tea . . . if you'd mind to come in fer a cup."

"Thank you. I'd like that." Kate lifted the broken gate and squeezed through following Mattie to her door; they entered and the small pail of water was set on the nearby washstand. Stepping inside Kate glanced about her. It was a small kitchen, dominated by the big black range with its blue enameled doors. Across the room was a tall glass-doored cupboard with a large butter bowl on top, a low armless rocker beside it. And over it on two sturdy pegs lay a small rifle. Robert's 22? In the center of the kitchen was a sturdy oak table with both leaves up. Kate stepped over to it. "What a lovely table!" She caressed the top with her fingertips.

"Bought thet fer a li'l o' nothin' when we first come here. I jest got through reddin' up some quilt blocks from it."

"Do you make quilts, too?"

"Mostly in the winter when the nights is long an' lonesome. Can't tend my flowers." Mattie was poking up the fire under the freshly filled small copper teakettle."Go on in to the front room an' set. I'll show you a coupl'a my quilts."

Kate passed through the low narrow doorway and surveyed that room. The large piano, old but polished to a shine, seemed to fill the room, dwarfing even the tall, black round heating stove, which now had a pot of ivy on top, sending green tendrils down over the little isinglass squares on the door. Other than that there were two rocking chairs and a library table covered with a long fringed runner, an old leather-bound Bible in the center. Kate looked at the photographs on top of the piano. One was a youngish mother with a smiling child of perhaps two on her lap. Yes, it must be Mattie with Robert. The small heart shaped face of the woman bore a slight resemblance. There were curls around her face and a bloom or sparkle making her quite attractive. The baby was beautiful with curly hair and big eyes.

Kate sat in one of the rockers and Mattie went to the little bedroom off to one side, opened a cupboard and took out two bundles wrapped in unbleached muslin. She carefully unwrapped them, partially unfolded the quilts, then spread them across the opposite rocker.

"Mattie, those are beautiful."

The old woman came close to smiling. "I been thinkin' I'd give you one or t'other, if you'd like it."

"Like it? I'd love it! Do you know I just papered that front bedroom upstairs with paper in a pattern of purple clover blossoms? I can't think of anything nicer to go with it than this one." She went over and picked up the corner of the quilt which had light green swirls on a darker green background with tiny pink and white blocks tucked in here and there.

"It's your'n then."

"Thank you so much! The other one is just as beautiful, but this happens to match my room."

After the quilts were rewrapped, Mattie sat down rocking slightly as though nervous. They talked about the cooler weather with a hint of fall and exchanged news about their most recent flower blooms. Then the hissing of the teakettle sent Mattie to the kitchen.

After a few minutes she returned with a plate for each of them containing tea in a big white old fashioned cup, scalloped frescoes around its flat bottom. A big brown cookie with raisins in the middle lay along side it. Kate smiled, "I finally told Ivan we'd met. Do you know what he remembers most about you? Your gingerbread and sorghum cookies."

"Well, land sakes take him home some then. I baked mor'n I can eat." She looked past Kate out the window as though remembering. "He always was the quiet one. The other two, the bigger boy an' the girl, they sometimes quarreled, but thet little tyke would jest come in the kitchen an' look 'round with his big, blue eyes. Follered Robert," Mattie's voice trembled, "like he id'lized him."

Kate's eyes were misty to hear her husband described as a boy. "He's still a good, good man and such a wonderful husband."

"I always thought his pa was sech a good man, too." The harsh bitterness in her voice returned as she rocked nervously with a jerk.

Kate tasted the tea and bit into the mellow cookie. She could see why Ivan remembered them. "Mattie, Ivan told me all he knew about what took place at the time of Robert's death. He was only about ten years old, so he didn't know much of what was going on. No one would talk about it and he didn't dare ask. I think everyone concerned was ashamed of how they let you down or whatever they did."

"Hm-mp. Well, Art never had no call to go talkin' 'round to others what I told him in private."

Kate then related the story of the Sunday evening incident which Ivan had witnessed, emphasizing his father's anguish.

"I hope he suffered a plenty, lettin' thet story out after I begged him not to, so I been shut up here 15 years 'fraid to go out fer what folks is a thinkin' an' a sayin'."

"From what Ivan says, I don't think any kind of story did get very far around. Amos Walls knew, but he's dead. Ivan's father, too. I know Serena Rockwell pretty well by now, and she has never told me anything. Maybe it's like my mother used to tell me when I was embarrassed over something. She'd say, 'You're probably the only one thinking about it. Everyone else is too full of their own problems."

"The last person he shoulda took it to was thet lechrous old preacher! Comin' round here behind his wife's back thinkin' I'd lay fer him. Was me he was spiteful o', not what Robert did. Talk 'bout sinin'. His heart was black as eny. He wasn't fit to shine the boots o' the only man I ever loved."

Kate was shocked, but controlled her voice and expression. "Ivan said that pastor left soon after, as he remembers."

"He did, an' I pitied the next church as got him."

"Seems like a nice young minister at the church now. He's been out to see us a few times."

"Stopped in here onct, too. I told him I didn't have nothin' to do with thet church no more. Called me Mrs. Enders. Makes me wonder if what you say is true. Ain't many people knows 'bout it eny more."

"Even if they do, I'm sure they understand. With so many kids getting into trouble these days, there may be more parents than we realize worrying over something worse than your son's stealing a horse."

The old lady stopped rocking and sat upright. "Stole a horse! Is that what yer man said?"

"He said that's what he thought it was. I don't know where he got his information."

"Nan probably told the kids thet to get 'em side-tracked." Mattie began the jerk-rocking again as though she was trying to make a decision. The tea was finished; they had set the plates on the library table.

"I jest think I'll tell ya the straight of it, so Ivan won't think too bad o' him. Somehow it jest don't seem so bad no more, good boy as he was. If he jest hadn't a gone to thet awful place an' got killed . . ." She pulled a handkerchief from her apron pocket, covered her face and sobbed miserably. Then to Kate's utter surprise, she suddenly got up, dropped her handkerchief and moved to the piano. Without a word, she sat down and started pounding. Kate recognized the hymn, "Work For the Night is Coming." She didn't know if it was her cue to leave or to sit and listen. She had said she was going to tell the story and had called Ivan by name for the first time. She'd wait. When she'd played through the chorus, Mattie got up from the piano bench and moved back to the rocker. "That ol' pie-anna has had to git me through a heap o' things." Kate nodded and smiled with compassion.

Mattie was calmed now and began her story. "There was this huckster wagon come through here with a fella named Clint. That's all I ever knew 'bout him. He seemed to be sellin' everthing from horse liniment to . . . books. He'd talk to Robert, hardly ever to me. It got so he was stoppin' 'bout ever day, sayin' he was jest on his route. Would stop 'long the road next to the field where Robert was a workin', takin' up his time.

"Well, Robert didn't hardly have no friends, 'cept the Anderson younguns, and they was way litt'ler. I always hoped he'd find a girl, marry an' give me some grandchildren. Anyways I told this Clint fella to come around in the evening. I'd cook him an' Robert some supper thinkin' that wouldn't waste so much of the day hours."

Mattie took another deep breath with a catch in it and continued: "First it did my heart good to see them a laughin' and talkin', pullin' jokes on each other. Then Robert asked me if it would be all right if Clint slept in the barn 'stead o' over at the park in his huckster wagon – had a bunk right in it. I said it was all right fer awhile, but by then I was beginnin' to wish he'd git through around here and move on."

"How old was he?" Kate's mind was racing ahead of the story and she wanted to slow it up, not sure she wanted to hear it all.

"He was mebby eight-ten years older'n Robert who was 20. Well, it was 'bout thet time he was a beggin' me to git him some o' thet money in his fund was due him when he was 21. Said Clint knew quite a lot about chemistry an' he was awful close to inventin' a dope to put on difrent crops to save weedin'. Something that'd leave the onions alone and kill the weeds. Sprinkle it right on. I said thet was just come-on talk, couldn't be no sech thing as thet. Then he said, 'Ma, medicine and pills is chemicals. If they git to yer insides and can figure out which part to go to, why can't chemicals sprayed on plants do the same?' Anyways I didn't help him git any of thet money.

"Clint spent several nights here. Robert said he'd sleep out there too, sted of the day bed I used to keep in here." She indicated where the library table now stood. "I could hear them out there till late a laughin' and carryin' on. Mornings got later and later till they come into breakfast long after Robert shoulda been in the field. Clint would apologize and leave money on the table for his meals, saying' it was so good 'n all."

Mattie rocked vigorously again, trying to keep calm. "On a Monday when I went to do my washin' and went to the barn to git Robert's overalls where he'd left 'em. Under 'em I found a book . . ." She made a face like tasting strong vinegar. "It had pitchers drawn in it like nothin' you'd believe. Men doin' things together worsen' animals." Her voice trembled uncontrollably, "And I knew Clint was lead'n him into doin' sech as thet."

"Oh, Mattie, that must have been a terrible shock!"

"Ain't no whay to describe what I felt. But when thet man came to drive away in his wagon, I threw thet book in the door an' said, 'Take this nasty book an' git your filthy self away from this place and Robert!' Well, he got out of here in a hurry, but I saw him stop and talk to Robert along the fence. I was jest ready to take the gun an' shoot over his head when he finally drove on.

"Robert hardly spoke to me fer the next few days. I don't know fer sure whether he was mad at me or jest ashamed. Spent his time outdoors, went on sleepin' in the barn and ate his meals without talkin'. Well, come Sunday mornin' they wanted me to play at church. Robert wouldn't go with me, so I rode over with Art and Nan. When I got back there was a note out there on the table said . . . 'don't worry 'bout me, I'll be back.' Then he wrote thet he had took $10 from the sugar bowl, thet he figured belonged to him." Mattie paused again. She was talking slower now and seemed in control.

"Takin' the $10 was all right. I wish't he'd taken a hundret, if it had been there. But I knew he was leavin' with or joinin' up with that Clint. Wern't much I could do but wait and wonder what I could do to ker-rect a 20-year-old boy. I never did believe in strappin' and I knew he was too big for thet anyways."

"Did you think of sending the sheriff after them?"

"I didn't want to do thet or it would be in the papers an' everwhere. But if I had to do it over, I woulda. I had no idea where Clint came from or where he was headed. Finally after two weeks an' I heard nothin', I couldn't stand it no longer. I was havin' a terrible time keepin' up the chores an' all. I knew he couldn't be livin' on jest $10. Thought mebbe he was stranded somewhere an' couldn't get back . . . too proud to let me know.

"So I made the mistake of goin' to Art fer help. Told him and Nan jest what I'm a tellin' you. He had no idea either where to find him, but he said he'd ask around of some o' the other farmers who mighta bought something from Clint and had an address on it. I begged him," Mattie's voice rose again, "to not tell nobody what Robert was led into an' he said he wouldn't. But I knew later he had, after Robert's body came back and I tried to make funeral arrangements for him at the church."

"Do you suppose, Mattie, that maybe he didn't tell? Maybe those who knew found out some other way, saw them together or maybe this Clint was selling his dirty books to other boys and their folks found out? They surely saw his huckster wagon here so often."

"I thought of thet, too, but no I think t'was Art. He looked an' acted too guilty when him an' ol' Amos came out here with thet preacher a snivelin' an' apologizin', quotin' Bible verses an' sayin' they couldn't allow the funeral in the church. They shoulda made thet preacher come alone. I'd o' shot him full of holes. I'd a been in prison, but thet's where I been anyway."

Kate wanted to ask why the poor bedeviled woman didn't move out of the community, but asked instead, "What did Robert die of, so suddenly?"

"Was knifed. Don't know much else. The sheriff here told me . . . from what he gathered, it happened in a bawdy roomin' house in Chicago. Died right off . . . no time to suffer . . . my only consolation. I wisht a thousand times I'd a helped him git some o' thet money if he was a bound to go an' find out about thet crazy weed killer. He coulda at least had a decent place to stay. He didn't know nothin' 'bout what goes on in cities."

"Where did you finally hold his funeral?"

"Didn't have no funeral a'tall. The undertaker from Morriston thet took care of his body suggested a preacher over there might come fer his burial. He brought a few o' his church people with him, and some as knew Robert around here came. Thet preacher was real nice. Come back to see me a few times b'fore he retired an' moved away. Which I 'preciated, 'cause them next weeks after buryin' him was the worst of my life, and I ain't had an easy one. Besides bein' numb from grief and shame, I had to find someone to run the farm. At least I had my horse and buggy then to go over to the graveyard real often, but it got so it wasn't safe on the roads no more. Now I jest sit here awaitin' out my time till I'm called. Can't even git to the cemetery but two, three times a year when the Rockwells take me."

"Why, you know I'd take you anytime!"

"I sure would be much obliged. It'd be quite a bit outta yer way goin' to town, but how I would like to go oftener. To jest see how things is a growin'... an' be there close to him."

"I'll pick you up tomorrow afternoon, whether I need to go to town or not. And Ivan and I will pick you up for other things, too. No use of you sitting here. You have a right to this community as much as anyone. You just keep telling yourself that. From what both you and Ivan say, Robert was a fine boy. Keep remembering that, too."

Kate stood up. "I really must go home now and start something for Ivan's supper. He'll be coming in hungry. I'd love to take him one of your cookies for a surprise though. And my quilt." She picked it up and hugged it.

Mattie took out a bread wrapper from a kitchen drawer, opened the stone jar, took out four big cookies and placed them in it. She said nothing more till Kate turned at the door to add another thanks and a goodbye. Gentle tears were streaming down Mattie Enders sallow cheeks. No sobs this time. "Dear girl . . . you'll never know . . . what yer doin' fer me. Ever since the time I come down to name yer posies, I began to feel a li'l like livin' 'gain. Like mebbe I was still some use to somebody. The good Lord musta finally answered my prayers when he stopped yer wheels in fronta my house thet day. I felt so bad later on thet I hollered at ya like thet."

Kate laughed. "Oh, I've almost forgotten about that. I'll pick you up about two tomorrow." Half way across the field she turned back and waved again to the old neighbor still watching her. The bond between Mattie and Kate was cemented. All those impulses she followed where it concerned Mattie – were they divinely inspired? What a beautiful feeling! She could hardly wait to report to Ivan, but she'd save it to go with the cookies for dessert.

She hadn't heard all the story yet. The trouble of 15 years ago was cleared up. But what of Robert's father? Was he that "only man she ever loved?" And what was the fund Robert was trying to get to? She had a feeling she'd hear it all someday.

CHAPTER 17

Filling The Silo

"WE'RE FIRST IN LINE for silo-filling this year!" Ivan announced coming into the kitchen where Kate was ironing. She looked up startled. "I stopped by Rocky's on the way home. He said here was as good a place to start as any. We've got to get all the way around before frost hits the corn. He'll bring the cutter down tomorrow and we'll get ready to start early Thursday morning."

"Thursday of *this* week! How can I be ready by then? I haven't even decided on a menu yet."

"Now don't worry about making a menu. They don't want anything fancy. Bake some beans and we'll get a ham or something. Just make plenty of whatever it is. They're a hungry bunch by dinner time."

Kate could see that Ivan was looking forward to silo-filling. It was hard work, he'd said, but they had a lot of fun out of it too, going from farm to farm, one after the other. And each cook trying to outdo the last. That innocent remark made Kate uneasy. Now she knew the dinner was what all the men looked forward to and the best cooks in the community would be competing, even Mrs. Rockwell.

"How many men will there be?" she asked calmly, not revealing her nervousness.

"I'm going around now to see the fellows in the ring so I can tell you better when I get back. But there will be 12 to 15." Kate winced, but said nothing. "Go to town tomorrow and buy whatever you need for that many or more. We won't worry about the expense this time."

After he'd gone out, Kate wondered if he thought she was so foolish as to prepare only half enough food. There would be plenty, but not a pile of leftovers to throw away. She didn't like waste.

So absorbed with thoughts of the dinner, Kate didn't realize her iron had gone cold until she flicked it with a dampened finger and it didn't even sizzle.

"Darn these irons!" she muttered and thought about her electric iron, a wedding present, stored upstairs. Clicking off the handle to the cold iron, she replaced it on a hot one, which had been heating over a burner on the kerosene stove.

That evening after the dishes were done, she worked out her menu while Ivan sat reading the paper under the lamp on the other side of the kitchen table.

He looked up and watched her busily going through a cookbook, writing and erasing. "Now, honey, you're not serving a tea room luncheon, you know. Why work so hard over it?"

"For goodness sake, Ivan, are you afraid I'm going to serve those men tea and toast?"

"Oh, now, I was only kidding. But I don't like to see you wearing yourself out over it before you even start the meal. Mrs. Rockwell will help you, I know, and there will be several other women offering to come along."

"But the planning is still up to me, right? So let me do it my way. Don't expect me to start in on a pile of groceries Thursday morning and have a big dinner whipped up by noon."

Thursday morning came and the two Andersons were up by daylight with a big and busy day ahead of them. Kate had gone to bed early, knowing she couldn't afford to be tired or sick to start the day. She had been feeling better since the advent of cooler weather and was seldom nauseated.

For the menu she had finally decided on baked ham, escalloped potatoes, baked beans, green beans with onion and bacon, fruit Jello, a relish plate of sliced tomatoes, celery and pickles, hot biscuits, chocolate cake, iced tea and coffee. It was all planned on paper, what time each item was to be prepared or put into the oven and when it should come out. This sheet, she carefully hid so that neither Ivan nor the women who came would see it.

There would be just the three of them to get the meal. Serena Rockwell and Ida Bryce were coming. Two other neighbors had called and told Kate if she needed them they'd miss the missionary society meeting and come. But Kate told them she was having an easy dinner and didn't need a lot of help. Frankly, she didn't want too many cooks to manage. Ida Bryce would be enough to get in her hair.

The Bryces' farm was west of the Andersons' a couple of miles. Bill Bryce graduated from high school in the same class with Ivan and married Ida the same year. They had no children. Bill was a serious but likeable, hard-working fellow. Kate couldn't say as much for his wife. She, too, was hard-working, doing all the chores in the busy season so that Bill could work later in the fields. She often helped in the field as well. But her house was usually a mess, or so it seemed to Kate the few times she'd been in it. Ida was always "just going to red-up this house." She was short and plump with dark-brown straight hair, pinned flat against her face. She talked too loud and laughed too often, but Kate was determined to get on with her since she was the wife of one of Ivan's close friends. They covered each other's chores when one or the other had to be gone.

Kate secretly hoped neither helper would come too early. She wanted to get her regular work done first and herself organized for the dinner preparation. It was an idle wish, for after Rocky came Bill, and Ida was with him. Kate met her at the door, coffee cup in hand.

"Uh-oh, Kate, you're as bad as me, sittin' around drinking coffee instead of doing your dishes."

Kate managed a laugh. "This is my second coffee. I had the first at five o'clock." She poured Ida a cup, then started picking up the dishes.

"Sit down, Kate, we got hours before noon. If Serena Rockwell's coming, we won't need to do anything anyway. She can get the dinner twice as fast in half the time." Another loud laugh.

Kate sat down opposite her for a moment, then got up again to resume the dishwashing. After several minutes and a lot of idle chatter, Ida got up also and dumped her cup, dregs and all, into the dishwater. "Now you get out, I'll wash these few dishes."

Kate murmured a thank you, dried her hands and went to make the bed and pick up the living room. When she returned, Ida was washing the milk pails and strainer in the same water in which she'd washed the greasy skillet. Kate made a mental note to rewash and scald them after Ida had gone home.

Kate put the dried dishes in the cupboard and secretly admired the two near-perfect chocolate cakes which sat there. She had spent all yesterday afternoon on them and they were to be the crowning of her dinner. Using her mother's recipe she'd made one, deciding if it didn't turn out she'd set it aside and think of something else for dessert. It turned out nicely, so she made another in order to serve generously. Now there the two cakes sat, side by side, tender and moist, rich and gooey, with a thick chocolate filling and chocolate icing. She never knew a hearty-eating man yet who didn't go for that chocolate cake.

To keep Ida from following her around talking every minute, Kate asked her if she wanted to peel potatoes. Ida agreed and Kate went to the cellar and brought up what seemed like enough potatoes for twenty men.

"Gracious, girl, you'll need half again that many. You've got lots to learn about feeding a hungry gang of silo-fillers. Ha. Ha. Ha. Not that I want to peel that many. Ha. Ha. Ha."

Against her better judgment, Kate went again to the cellar and brought up four more large potatoes and laid them in the pan of water where Ida was starting to peel.

By the time they had the potatoes sliced, prepared and in the oven along side of the ham, Serena Rockwell arrived. "You're having ham and scalloped potatoes, I see," she said cheerfully. "That's always good and not so much work at the last minute. I'm having chicken tomorrow, so I hoped you wouldn't have that."

"No danger," Kate laughed, "slow as I am at cleaning just one."

The older woman put on her cover-up apron and looked around, wordlessly summing up the situation, seeing where her neighbor needed help and where she didn't. Ida still continued to chatter, thrusting in her jabs here and there, but now they worried Kate less. Serena Rockwell was a steadying influence.

"I thought maybe you'd make the biscuits for me," Kate said to her.

"Why sure. Glad to. I'll make and cut them now and they can set where it's cool until time to bake them." She went to the cabinet, got out a large bowl and started winding down flour through the built-in sifter.

Kate and Ida stretched out the dining room table, laid the cloth and set it. Noise from the barn proved that the silo-filling was in full progress. Ivan hadn't been in the house since breakfast.

As noon drew nearer, Kate couldn't refrain from getting more and more nervous. To her the dinner was an important debut. All the wives would be asking what did she have? Was it good? Did she have enough? She slipped away from Ida and went to the bedroom to check her list and see that nothing had been forgotten. How she'd like to lie down on that bed for just a few minutes! Instead she took a handful of crackers and showed them to Mrs. Rockwell while Ida was in the dining room. Serena nodded knowingly as Kate headed for the cellar to get the jars of green beans. She sank down at the little table and put her head on her arms for a few minutes, then ate the crackers. When she returned with the beans, Ida called out, "Oh, there you are! I thought you'd gone to the barn or something." Laugh, laugh, laugh.

Smiling wanly Kate handed her the beans to open. When she had them in a pan on the stove she said, "I suppose I could cut the pie and cake."

"Cake, Ida, but not pie," Kate said cheerfully, thinking again of the two waiting beauties, which she wasn't anxious for Ida to whack into.

"Ah-oh, you're in for a razzin', you are, if those men don't get their pie!"

Kate's heart sank. All morning she had been shrugging off Ida's jabs, but this one struck. Perhaps because it had occurred to her when she was making her menu that at most places they had been for a meal more than one dessert was served. That was the reason for the rich chocolate cake – it would surely be enough to finish off the meal. But now she wondered would it seem like enough? She looked to Serena for consolation.

"Oh, now, Ida, there's places they don't have both." She sounded like she was trying to think of someplace. "But if you want me to, Kate, I can have pies made and in the oven in no time." She said it as casually as though there was still time to make the coffee.

Kate was stunned. Clearly they both thought she should have pie. "After all those biscuits you made? I couldn't ask you to do that. It's 11 o'clock!"

"Nonsense. Go grab me two jars of peaches. I'll make three pies and they can be cooling over a pan of water while they eat the first part of the meal." She was already whirling down more flour into the biscuit bowl.

Kate dashed again for the cellar. She must keep her mind occupied or she'd break into tears any minute now. Would this dreadful day never end? Having silo-fillers fun!?! Had she said that once upon a time?

Kate pulled out the rubber seal on the jars of peaches and got them ready for Serena, who was calmly giving Ida orders: "Poke up the fire . . . take those potatoes out of the oven, they're done . . . put in the biscuits. They'll bake in a few minutes . . . Kate can finish cutting the ham. No one will ever know these are last minute pies."

In spite of the turmoil in her mind, Kate couldn't help but marvel at the way that woman worked. She hardly looked hurried, yet the huge mound of flour was instantaneously taking the form of pastry. She wasted not one motion. She sprinkled in salt and the water with her left hand as she crumbled the flour and lard with her right. She reached for the rolling pin with her right hand as she squeezed off a piece of dough with her left. Kate imagined that both Ivan's mother and grandmother had been cooks like that. And he's stuck with me, she thought miserably.

"Now where's the pie pans?" Serena asked.

Kate left the coffee-making and ran for them, then remembered she had only two. She handed them to Serena and hurried about looking for the glass pie plate around somewhere. On her schedule, this was the time to be setting the men's wash water out on a bench in the backyard as Ivan had instructed. And there was still the ham to finish cutting. Ida was noisily stirring the green beans again. If she didn't stop, they would be soup. She hammered the spoon on the edge of the pan with a clatter. How could Bill stand her day after day!?!

The intermittent hum and drone at the barn stopped and Kate could hear the loud talking and laughing closer to the house now. Ida shouted. "Better get your wash water out, Kate. They're coming." As though it wasn't obvious that was what she was doing.

Ida poured iced tea into the glasses while Serena and Kate dished up bowls of food. The older woman was still completely unruffled. Another day of this for her tomorrow – and how many more?

One by one the men came in from washing, through the kitchen to the dining room, pulled chairs back from the table and seated themselves, more quietly now, to wait for the others. Many of them Kate didn't recognize, but she spoke to all as they walked through. She caught a glimpse of Ivan, changing the wash water for each man, waiting till last to wash himself. He smiled reassuringly in at her as though he could see everything was under control. Little did he know!

The men ate heartily, constantly laughing or joking, but with no comment about the food. Kate hovered over the table, refilling dishes, pouring more tea and coffee. Mrs. Rockwell kept up with the work in the kitchen. Ida stood around nibbling off this and that.

When most of the men looked as though they were ready for dessert, Kate went to bring the cakes. "We'll let the pies cool as long as possible," she said to Serena. She was at least going to have the consolation of serving them before Serena's lovely pies. The cakes now looked very commonplace. She handed one to the man at the end of the table and set the other on the buffet. Ivan had outlawed any extra serving dishes on the table, even for dessert. It seemed messy to her, but if using dessert plates was "putting on airs" why bother.

The very large man who held the cake took out a piece with the point of his knife, steadied it with his thumb and held it in mid air. "Say man, look at that cake! Frosting a half-inch thick."

The cake went around the table with every man making some comment, except Ivan who merely beamed.

"My cook's been at it for 30 years and she can't make a cake like that – anyway she don't."

"I tell my wife sometimes, it looks like she ran out of frosting when she makes a cake. Never puts any on the sides. Boy, I like plenty of frosting!"

"Ive, you old fox, I thought you married this gal for her looks, and here she can cook, too."

It was Kate's moment. She laughed with them, but kept in the background, trying to remain very modest and wifely, not daring to look at Ivan. When the cake had gone around, she went to bring the pies and realized she felt no longer tired. The pies did seem anti-climax, but all ill-feeling over them was forgotten.

Rocky said, "Here, Bill, you eat the pie. I can have that at home anytime." Then he whispered loudly, "I see another cake over there and I'm going to have another piece if she offers it to me."

"Can't eat another bite," Bill said. "Here, Henry, you start it. It's still warm, even." The first of the three pies went around the table with only four pieces taken. Kate brought the other cake and some of the men who'd passed up the pie slipped off another piece of cake.

The last man left the house and the noise at the barn started up again. Serena had set the kitchen table with three places and Kate sank into a chair laughing. "Well, it's over. I guess getting dinner for silo-fillers isn't so bad afterall."

"I should think not with all those compliments," Serena said, smiling. "We don't all rate that kind of talk, you know. At least till they get home."

"This is good cake. I got that much to say." For once Ida didn't laugh as she finished the piece of cake she'd been picking at.

Kate wanted Serena to go right home after eating, since she had to get ready for her dinner the following day. But she wouldn't think of leaving till the dishes were done. Then, much to Kate's relief, she offered to take Ida home so she wouldn't have to wait for Bill. Ida readily agreed. She could get the chores done since Bill would be late.

As they were leaving, Kate said, "I'll be up to help you tomorrow, Serena, but it won't be the kind of help you gave me. And thank you, Ida." She handed them each a pie wrapped in wax paper. "Here take home a souvenir of the day's work for your suppers." She had the fleeting thought that she should be handing Ida a dish of those leftover cold potatoes.

"We didn't need the pies after all, did we?" Serena said, as though it had just occurred to her.

After they left, Kate wandered outdoors to get some fresh air and to see what she could of the silo-filling. Everyone, especially Ivan, looked too busy to explain anything. He merely looked up and raised his eyebrows in greeting. But she could see that, just as he'd told her previously, the cornstalks were being pushed into the narrow shoot with the conveyer which sent them into the chopping apparatus. Then the shredded fodder was blown up through a long slender pipe with a curve at the top, into the silo, where it would ferment and become nutritious cow "sauerkraut."

Kate shuddered, watching Ivan constantly pushing the corn from the waiting wagon into the cutter. What would happen to an arm if it should get caught and carried along with the stalks? She hoped that wouldn't be Ivan's job at every farm they went to.

On her way back to the house, she noticed the chickens hungrily picking in the dirt outside the hen house. She went to the corn crib and cranked a pail of ear corn through the sheller, then scattered it for them. She carried water to fill their pan and gathered the eggs. Ida was going home to do all of Bill's chores, bringing in the cows and milking them. All the things Kate had no idea how to do and would be frightened to try.

There was, in spite of her original intention, a mountain of leftovers to choose from, so supper wasn't much of a chore. There would still be many scraps to go into the pail where the suitable garbage was kept for hog feed.

"You took care of the chickens, didn't you?" Ivan said as he finally came in looking very, very tired. "It's a good thing, or they would have gone to bed hungry tonight."

"Ida went home early to do all of Bill's chores," Kate remarked as she set the warmed leftovers on the table.

"Poor Bill, he was worn right down to the nubs tonight. I thought that hand of Cooper's was heavy enough on his feet to be good inside the silo tramping it down, but Bill said tonight he didn't do much but lean up against the silo, smoke and talk. If he'd told me that at noon, I'd have put someone else in there with Bill and had him take a team. But good old Bill, he never complains. Rocky and I decided tonight we'd tell Jim he has to send a hand who's worth something."

"Was his hand that big fellow at this end of the table who started talking about the cake?"

"Yeah, that's him. Say, that was good cake. Is that what you were doing all yesterday afternoon?" Kate laughed and nodded. "Well, they made me promise to ask you to make another one to celebrate the last day of silo filling. They want to buy ice cream to go with it. It will be a short day at Bill's anyway. He doesn't have a very big silo." After a pause he added, "You know what kind of a meal we'll get out of Ida anyway, don't you?"

Kate looked up in surprise. She supposed Ida would go all out. She had been bursting with things about Ida to report to Ivan, but she didn't feel like saying them now. It was just Kate's initiation to silo-filling. Next year she'd quietly insist on using her own judgment about the dinner, no matter who came to help.

CHAPTER 18

Love Story

IVAN HELD HIS ONION CROP as long as he dared, in crates in the barn where they sat tier upon tier. He couldn't chance the market too long; it could go down as well as up. In the recent past years, some farmers had been unable to sell their onions at any price and ended up dumping them back on the field to be plowed under.

The dry onions had been pulled and laid in windrows, then topped with special shears and dropped into crates, which were hauled to the barn and under cover. Every onion farmer feared a heavy rain before his crop was in.

To get the onions ready for market, more hand work was required. Each crate was emptied onto the wooden-slated table screen and the onions were pushed along by hand to the shoot at the lower end where a burlap bag was hooked. The onions smaller than one and one-half inch and the loose hulls dropped through to be discarded. Ivan sadly saw too much of his crop falling through the cracks and resolved that someday he'd find a way to market those small onions.

Each 50 pound sack was sewed shut with a curved needle threaded with twine. Then the crop was hauled into Richland and loaded on a freight car assigned to a wholesaler in Chicago.

Ivan opened the letter containing the check in return. He looked at it solemnly and, with a sigh, showed it to Kate.

Kate glanced at it and murmured, "Uh-huh," and continued washing the kitchen windows. Was this the pay check that was to put them in gear after coasting along on milk checks all summer? It wasn't much more than enough to make the yearly payment at the bank. She should have realized after the kind of summer they'd had, but still, she'd hoped.

"Want to go along into town to take it to the bank?"

"No, I think not today. I want to finish these windows. But remember to get a loaf of bread." She needed to be alone with her thoughts for awhile.

Ivan left without further comment. She saw the car disappear up the lane. After finishing the windows, she threw the towels on the back porch. Work, work, work. What did it bring them? Just another day of planning how to spend every nickel. She went outdoors, slamming the kitchen door behind her, picked up a trowel from the wood shed window sill and absently began digging in the chrysanthemums. Where was the enthusiasm she had when first they came to this "quaint old farm?"

When Ivan returned, Kate was still digging and transplanting. He walked slowly towards her. She looked up. From the grocery bag he awkwardly handed her a pound box of Whitman's chocolates, her favorite. "I guess this looks kind of silly out of a whole onion crop. But it's a token of the big things I'd like to give you – and how much I love you."

She stood up and kissed him; he took her in his free arm. "How much I love you, too, you old sweetheart," she said. "Thank you for the candy. My blues over the small check didn't last long after I began digging in the good old earth. Don't worry about me, darling, or the farm either. It was a hard summer, but we had happy days mixed in."

"Anyway, I did go ahead and buy paint for the house. I can get it on during the good days before bad weather sets in."

"Oh, good! Did you get that shade we looked at?"

"Dove gray, wasn't it?" Kate nodded and they stepped back looking at the house, picturing how it would look with its new coat of paint.

After Ivan had gone on out to the barn "to finish cleaning it before chore time" he'd said, Kate's thoughts turned to Mattie Enders. Digging in the chrysanthemums, she had tried to dwarf her small problems beside the kind Mattie had. She now looked at her watch. Not yet 3 o'clock and they were having sausage gravy, sweet corn and tomatoes for supper. She'd have time to take Mattie over to the cemetery yet this afternoon. Since Mattie's request, Kate had been taking her over twice a week.

Ivan had been most interested in the rest of Mattie's story about Robert. He couldn't remember where the "stolen horse" idea came from. Maybe he and Claud just imagined it. He was as shocked as Kate at the real situation. And yes, he remembered the huckster wagon with a bed right in it, shelves lined with merchandise. "I never did see any of those books, though." Kate shot him a bemused frown. "They might have been interesting. Worse than animals, huh?"

Yes, she would. She'd call Mattie and they'd both go work at the cemetery. Kate rang the short and the long now without caring who listened in. "Hello, Mattie, how about a trip to the cemetery this afternoon? I'll go and weed, too."

"Sure. Jest soon as I shut down the stove an' git my sleeves on an' tools gathered up. Toot when you git here."

Kate left a note for Ivan in case he came in before she returned. On the way up the lane she smiled, thinking how Mattie enjoyed these trips. Who would dream anyone could get such pleasure from trips to the cemetery? But she loved flowers and she loved Robert. They were both there for her.

The last time Kate had taken her, it was on the way into town. When she returned, Mattie had finished her "flower tendin' " and was just sitting, her head leaned against the lovely brown marble stone with Robert's name chiseled on it. Kate had parked at the gate and walked over. Mattie didn't hear her coming. Her sunbonnet was pushed back, making the ruffles around her face resemble the curls in the picture on her piano. There was a bit of the glow that was evident in the picture. She looked years younger with the soft expression. Of what was she thinking? Heaven and Robert? Or that mysterious man – the only one she ever loved?

Mattie was waiting outside. "I thought some digging and weed pulling today might help me bury some of my troubles," Kate said as they drove.

"What's a settin' heavy on yer mind?"

"Oh . . . I guess it doesn't seem like much to anyone else, but I'd counted so much on having a bathroom before winter. We got our onion check today and it's not much more than enough to cover the bank note. That's pretty small potatoes beside your troubles, isn't it?"

"No t'aint. You been used to a bathroom. Not like us out here in the country grew up without. An' you havin' a baby an' all." After a pause she added. "Don't know as I kin do no more 'bout yer troubles than you kin mine. But a body kin set an' listen." Kate marveled again at the wisdom of this lady.

They drove into the cemetery and parked under the trees. Mattie got out and stood just looking around for a few minutes. "It's always so purty an' peaceful here, I jest wait for the day I kin be laid out here a side Robert under these here ol' pine trees."

"It is lovely here," Kate agreed.

There was little they could do around Robert's grave except water the flowers, so they decided to work on other nearby neglected graves which bothered Mattie. Both heads now bent over the weeding, Kate said, "Ivan felt so bad for me, more than himself, I think, because of the small onion check. He brought me a box of candy, the first since we've been married."

"Them presents means a lot. My man used to slip li'l surprises in on my table onct in awhile."

"Did you say you've never been married, Mattie, or just not to Robert's father?"

"No, I never been married, but I did a lot o' pretendin' an' was more faithful than some thet has."

"I don't mean to be nosey, but Ivan said Robert was such a nice looking boy. His father must have been a handsome man."

"Oh, he was. An' I don't mind telling ya about him if you're a mind to hear."

"I'd love to hear the story."

"Well, after my ma died, my pa had been dead fer years, and she was bedrid fer a couple years before she went. That's when I learned to play the pieanna, from a music teacher I did some sewin' fer. My sisters had all moved away an' I didn't wanta stay there on thet place. It was jest a li'l Kentucky hill patch, grew some corn and sorghum cane, like thet. So I sold it fer what I could git. But before thet I got real nervy and put a ad in the Lexington paper thet I was experienced in home nursing and house work. I was in my thirties then, not young. First thing I knowd I got this answer on fancy paper from a horse farm. Got some other answers, too, but none as invitin' as this one. I couldn't git on the bus and git over there fast enough.

"Girl . . . it was the most beautiful country place I ever dreamed about! White board fence all the way around the horse paddock an' up the lane on both sides. Green rollin' hills . . . I jest melted at the sight of it and wanted to work there worse then anything. The lady thet met me at the door was all dressed up in her ridin' britches and acted like she jest had to git somewheres in a awful hurry. She talked to me lessn' five minutes and said I was hired. She showed me the cabin where I was to stay, gave me a list o' things I was to be responsible fer, and they was a lot, then she left jest like thet. She said Nita, the colored girl, would show me where things wuz.

"Well, to make a long story short, thet woman's husband, Rowland, was Robert's father. Ol' Mrs. Sassafrass, as Nita and me called her behind her back, run thet farm thet had been her daddy's like Rowland didn't have eny part of it. She was a devil to anyone on two legs, but as kind and gentle to them horses as you could want. She'd set up all night with a horse ready to foal, but she wouldn't warm her husband's bed even one night a month."

Kate was so interested in this unbelievable story she was hearing, she could hardly keep on with the weeding as they moved from one spot to another.

"Right from the start, I had a beau," Mattie continued. "He worked on a farm close by. He was jest somebody to go places with, didn't mean much to me. But it didn't take me long to fall head over heels in love with thet Rowland. He was so kind and considerate. I kept a wonderin' how she could turn her back on him. But since she did, I welcomed him. We never got caught neither. When I found out I was in a family way, God forgive me, I didn't even feel shamed. I loved thet man so much and was so happy to have his baby no matter what become of us." She stopped her work and looked up. Kate could see again the love shining through.

"One day, later on, when I was beginning to show good, she said, 'Mattie, are you with child?' "

"I said, 'Yes, ma'm.' "

" 'Are you goin' to marry Simon?' she asked. That was my former beau."

" 'No ma'm,' "

" 'Well, yer a good worker.' It's the only compliment she ever gave me. 'Mabbe we can see you through this, if you can work right up to time and soon again after.' Then as she hurried away, as usual, she tossed back at me, 'Decide what you want to do with the baby.' "

Kate gasped. "What did she expect you to do with it?"

"I don't know what she expected, but there was never eny doubt in my mind what I would do. Rowland asked me if I wanted to leave and I told him, no, not unless he wanted me to."

"Then he said, 'Mattie, I don't ever want you to leave. You an' that li'l fella belongs to me an' I'm goin' to take care o' you.' "

"Thet made me so happy an' I worked so hard right along jest to be worthy o' him. He'd worry about me an' try to make things easier without her knowin' about it. Nita helped me a lot, too, an' when my time came, it was one of her relations knew about bringin' babies into the world an' Rowland went to fetch her. As luck would have it, ol' Mrs. S. was gone to a horse show. Rowland begged off goin' 'cause he knew it was my time. So fer four whole days he belonged to me an' Robert. Some other times, too, but this time I remember above all. He was jest as tickled as eny new father could be and nobody else knew it but Nita. She knew right from the start and kept still about it.

"Would you b'lieve when Mrs. S. come back from thet show an' Rowland told her I had the baby, she didn't pay no more mind then if he'd said the barn cat had kittens. She jest told Nita to take care o' me a li'l till I could git my strength back an' not be off work too long. In less then ten days I started in again, carryin' li'l Robert in a basket along side o' me. He was the best baby, jest suck his li'l ol' fist till I could nurse or change him. The Mrs. never looked in the basket even when she was close by. I was always afraid she would, he already looked so much like his pa.

"Things went along real good. Rowland still came to me when he could, but we was always mighty careful there warn't no more babies. Robert started to school, rode the school hack in. His teachers said he was smart, but a body could tell thet, the things he said and did."

"Did Mrs. Sassafras ever blame Simon for the baby or say he should help out financially?"

"No, Simon left fer another job somewheres long b'fore Robert was born."

"Now, I'm anxious to know when and why you left."

"Well, one day when Robert was nine years old, Mrs. S. said to me, 'Is that kid o' yers any good? Maybe it's time to put him to work.' He had been helpin' around quite a bit, follerin' his dad an' callin' him mister. Rowland talked to him a lot an' taught him things. I kept warnin' Robert to stay away from the Mrs. because she didn't like kids a'tall. An' he minded me.

"Then came the day when the Mrs. called Robert to her out in the barn lot. She sounded kind of pleasant like, the way she talked to her horses. I think she had in mind a specific job for him to do. He wasn't afraid of her, jest answered her with 'Yes, ma'm' an' 'No, ma'm.' Then from the cabin I saw her frown, take his chin in her hand, turn his head this way and thet, then she swung around and stomped off towards the house. I heard her shoutin' fer Rowland who'd jest gone in and then she bellered out, 'Git Mattie and thet God-damned son of yours off this place. I'll git me a maid that's so fat an' ugly you'll keep yer hands off her!' Thet's all I heard b'cause I started packin' to leave."

Kate couldn't suppress a little giggle, "I'm sorry. I think that's kind of funny – living under her nose for 10 years and she couldn't see him for the horses."

Beneath the sun bonnet, Mattie grinned broadly. "I had a few smiles out'ta thet myself."

"What happened after that outburst?"

"A coupla days and we was on our way up here. Rowland contacted a land agent thet found me this place and he bought it for us. Said there was onion weedin' fer the boy to do and we'd be quite comfortable. He said he'd take care of us an' his word was good as gold . . ."

Mattie sighed. "I guess I always kinda hoped he'd leave her and come to us. But thet didn't make no sense. He was a respected country gentleman down there, but here he'd be a nobody. So I never saw him agin after he put us on the train. He had thet land agent see thet we got picked up and brought out here. Nan and Art helped me out, too, gittin' started, buyin' a horse and a buggy and a li'l furniture. There was some already in the house. Awhile before Robert's trouble, we got word through a lawyer thet Rowland had died and there was some money willed to him when he turned 21. I was sure glad I'd sent a picture to him how Robert looked growed up. Didn't put no return address on it so the missus would know where it was from."

"Did Robert know who his father was?"

"After all the hollerin' from the Mrs. thet day an' us havin' to move out so sudden, I had to tell him all he could understand. I jest couldn't lie to him. He was tickled to death Mister Rowland was his daddy."

"Mattie, that is one of the most beautiful love stories I have ever heard!" They both stood up now, collecting tools and getting ready to leave.

As they walked to the car, Mattie again looked around the whole cemetery. "If you'd a mind to bring me over here some nice mornin' next week, I b'lieve I could finish cleanin' up this whole place b'fore winter sets in. I'll bring me some bread and cheese an' a thermos of coffee and a cookie and have lunch right there along side Robert."

As they drove away, Mattie said, "If you stop by the station, I'd like to fill up yer tank with gas."

"All right. I'll do that, even though it isn't necessary," Kate said absently. Her mind was still down on a horse farm in Kentucky. All that had happened to Mattie Enders? Who'd believe it! No wonder she wanted to stay right there in that house. It was all she had left of her Rowland.

CHAPTER 19

The Harvest

"IT'S GOING TO FROST TONIGHT," Ivan predicted as he came in after his morning chores and rubbed his hands over the warmth of the kitchen stove. "It's time to get the produce in from the muck garden. Do you want to come along this afternoon?"

"I wouldn't miss it!"

Right after dinner Ivan stopped by the house with the tractor idling and pulled Kate up beside him. The wagon followed as they bounced, tractor speed, to the muck garden near the lake. It had been planted to late summer and fall vegetables, then cultivated along with the field crops. Earlier they had eaten what they could of the sweet corn before it turned hard.

Ivan forked out the hills of potatoes and Kate helped pick them up. He pulled turnips and carrots, while she picked the last of the tomatoes. They left the pumpkins and squash until last and picked only what they thought they would use. Kate visioned them stacked along one side of the cellar. Finally she sat down wearily on an upturned onion crate and looked at the loaded wagon. "Imagine all this from those shriveled-up seeds we planted last spring!"

"The rains came in time to help the fall vegetables, at least." Ivan turned up another crate and sat down, a large turnip in his hand. He took out his pocket knife and started peeling, holding it by its top to keep it clean. He sliced off a chunk and handed it to Kate from the tip of his knife. "Here's your picnic lunch."

"How did you do that so neat?"

"That's a ritual, eating a turnip in the field after the last of the produce is gathered. I learned it from my dad and I suppose he learned it from his."

The turnip was cold and crisp. Kate marveled at how such a simple treat, while sitting out in the middle of a muck field, could bring so much pleasure. "Heaven's bounty," she murmured.

"Amen."

Kate sighed. "How Tommy would enjoy this."

"You haven't heard from him since the wedding, have you?"

"Just that printed thank you card, obviously from May Bell. I expect he's pretty busy adjusting to the routine of an office job after the freedom he's enjoyed from traveling."

"I can just hear you thinking – and adjusting to May Bell."

"Yes. Do you suppose I'm jealous of anyone marrying my brother? I worry about him, Ivan. He's so gullible and such a romantic. He always needed me to keep him down to earth."

"Now, I'm the one who benefits."

"With you I'm afraid it's the other way around." They rose and kissed, then with an arm about each other, they walked back to their wagonload of produce.

The following Sunday, Kate and Ivan went to church. It happened to be the week, once in about every two months, when the popular young minister, passed out to each family his hectographed news notes. It contained uplifting thoughts and Bible verses between the news items: who was sick or shut in and needed their prayers, what was scheduled at the church in the upcoming weeks, thank yous and so on. Ivan put it in his suit pocket and didn't read it until returning home later in the afternoon. They had gone directly to an Amish restaurant several miles distant. The meal was scrumptious and inexpensive.

While Kate was changing her clothes, Ivan sat reading the church bulletin. He called to her, "Kate, listen to this."

" 'Our thanks goes to sister Mattie Enders for her recent dedicated service to our little cemetery. Please stop by soon and see the wonders she has wrought. Older members will remember her at the piano several years ago. She is now using those talented hands in the service of our Lord at the cemetery.' "

Kate called Mattie immediately to see if she knew about the item. She laughed a pleasant little cackle. "Sakes alive, yes. The preacher stopped by with thet piece of paper yesterday and t'day the whole church musta' drove by the cemetery, all them calls I been gittin'. I didn't know I was doin' anything special. But it makes a body feel kinda proud."

Several frosts later, after all but the hardiest flowers had crumpled, Ivan came to wake Kate after the fires were built. "Get up, lazy bones, Jack Frost has been here again."

Kate was awake instantly, sat up and looked out. The roof tops and grass were glistening white. "Isn't it beautiful?"

He brought her robe and put it around her shoulders. "Come Sunday we can start gathering hickory nuts. They'll be falling fast now."

"Let's make a day of it and have a weenie roast!" She pulled the tangerine robe tight around her and shook stray hair out of her eyes.

"You and your picnics! Soon we'll be having them in the snow." He sat down and looked hungrily at her.

"Oh, shoo out of here and go do your milking. Breakfast will be ready soon." She pushed him off the bed with a quick kiss.

Sunday was a bright and beautiful day after another rain. Kate had the lunch ready before they went to church, all but the beans, which she left in the oven to finish baking.

While in the car and ready to go home, they saw Michelle Rockwell coming down the steps in new silk stockings and high heels. "Let's ask her to go with us," Kate said.

Shelly welcomed the invitation and by the time Kate and Ivan were home, changed and getting the lunch together, Shelly was also changed and coming down the lane.

The little woods was now a blaze of glory with its gold and scarlet leaves from the maples, hickory and oak. They chose a spot in a clearing, then Shelly made a circle of stones while Ivan gathered wood for a fire and Kate prepared the old camp coffeepot to hang over it. While it was heating and the fire burning to embers for roasting, they began gathering nuts.

Apart from them, Shelly was quickly and happily filling her pail. Ivan remarked quietly to Kate, "That's the same girl who has the reputation for always lagging behind in the onion field and hating every minute she's there." Later he insisted she keep separate all the nuts she'd gathered to take home with her. The afternoon went by pleasantly. Chore time came too soon.

Ivan wanted to look under one more tree in the far corner of the woods for nuts he remembered being extra large. Kate and Shelly settled down in the grass beside pails full of the little hard-shelled nuts. They began taking off outer hulls which had clung to some of the nuts. "You looked so pretty all dressed up in your new high heels this morning. New dress, too, wasn't it?"

"We were in Fort Wayne all day yesterday. I got a new Sunday dress, two new school dresses, new school shoes and some high heels that are my very own. Also some pretty under things." She hunched up her shoulders happily. "Clara and Mary's clothes don't fit me anymore, so I don't have to wear their handdowns."

Kate smiled at her obvious delight. She saw it so seldom in Shelly. "How's school this year?"

"Oh, I guess it's going to be all right." Then she added shyly, "Ive got a date for the carnival next Friday night."

"That's exciting! Maybe we'll see you there. Ivan bought tickets from a boy in town."

"I hope you win a cake or something. I'm going to work in the fish pond."

"Better I should visit the fish pond than the cake walk. I'm trying to keep from gaining too much weight."

"When is your baby due?"

"The last of March. Not too many people know about it yet, but they will soon."

Ivan returned with another full bucket and they began loading the car to return home.

On Tuesday of that week, Serena Rockwell urged Kate to go to an all day quilting bee with pot luck dinner. It was a fund raising project for the church and "We always have such a good time visiting over the quilt," she had said.

Ivan urged her to go also. He would be painting all day. Kate had helped him some days, mostly the white trim and what she could reach from the ground. As she quilted, she wished she were at home painting. Taking the tiny painstaking stitches bored her when the trivial conversation was about people she didn't know or events she hadn't attended. She was glad when she could excuse herself and go home to see how the painting was progressing.

As she drove in, Ivan, with a big grin, waved to her from the ladder. Going around the house to park in back, she realized the reason for his levity. He had painted the outhouse! First thing this morning, apparently, because he had already added touches of white trim and little stick figures racing across the top.

She laughed as Ivan came around to where she stood. "I thought I was supposed to be the decorator, and look at you with all this talent."

"I just do exteriors."

"Well, now just maybe I will do something to the interior. I'll have purple clover on one wall, red birds on another and finish with trailing ivy or whatever other scraps I've got left. We'll give people something to remember us by – our fancy privy."

CHAPTER 20

Ending Of A Feud

KATE SAT AT THE OLD TREADLE MACHINE sewing and mentally planning her maternity wardrobe. The dress she was making would do fine for dress-up occasions. She'd made some wrap-arounds to wear at home. For town and visiting, she'd made a skirt and remodeled an old dress into a top to go over it. Before they were married, she thought her clothes would last a year – but hadn't planned on such broad ones.

It was getting so dark she could hardly see. As she looked up, a few feathery flakes blew past the window. She jumped up, went closer to look and saw Ivan standing in the big open barn door also looking out. It was snow without a doubt! Leaving the half-finished garment hooked in the sewing machine, she grabbed her jacket from the wall hook by the kitchen stove and hurried out. She danced along towards the barn like a delighted child, but there was no secrecy about her pregnancy now.

"It's snowing!" she shouted at Ivan.

"Is it?"

"Isn't it heavenly?" She held up her face and hands to meet the white flakes.

"Oh, I don't know. I've seen it snow before."

"Not since I've been here."

"Is that supposed to make a difference?"

"Of course."

"I could have told you this morning it was going to snow."

"Why didn't you, then?"

"You didn't ask me. Besides, I was afraid you'd want to celebrate with a picnic."

They stood together in the barn door, facing the multiplying snowflakes in the early-gathering dusk. "Are you going to sleep in the hay mow tonight?" Ivan asked. "You haven't yet, you know."

"I've given up on that. You won't sleep with me."

"Then are you going to help me feed the chickens?"

"I'm not supposed to involve myself with farm work."

"But we have to teach that boy to be a farmer. We might as well start early."

"What if it turns out to be a girl?"

"I think it is. Come on."

After the chickens were fed and they'd gone into the kitchen to warm and add more wood to the fire, Kate went back with Ivan to feed the cows and do the milking. There was a light covering on the ground now.

The barn seemed warm and pleasant in the soft glow of the lantern light. The cows rattled their stanchions waiting for their supper. Kate watched while Ivan climbed up the narrow ladder to the top of the tall block silo, then forked the cows' winter food through a little door to a smelly heap below. Cow sauerkraut. The little doors were all in place when it was filled. Now they were removed one by one to the right level as the ensilage was removed.

Kate thought of how mysterious the inside of the empty silo seemed when Ivan first took her on a tour of the barn. Now that she'd been here through a silo-filling, she was beginning to feel like a real farm wife.

Kate went again to see the new red and white calf and was envious of the mother cow, that her waiting time was over. Then she milked her first cow. Perched on a three-legged stool beside what Ivan considered the gentlest animal in the herd, she clutched the milk pail between her knees. She pulled with both hands and expected to hear a zing on the bottom of the pail like when Ivan milked. But nothing came.

Ivan, standing close by, laughed heartily. "You're supposed to pull, then squeeze at the top, not the bottom."

After a few more attempts, she had a feeble stream of milk coming with each effort. It was fun but tiring. She listened to the hiss of milk squirting into Ivan's pail. How in the world did he manage to get six cows milked night and morning, seven days a week! When she had hardly more than a pint she gave up, her wrists aching.

"I think I'll go cook supper. I've found one thing I'm worse at than cooking." She hung her pail on the steel hook along the cement wall.

"Thanks for your help," Ivan called. She could hear him chuckling until she left the barn. Smiling with happiness, Kate walked slowly through the snow toward the warm-lighted kitchen.

It was an early snow and didn't remain long, but it started the rabbit hunting season. Rocky and Ivan, and sometimes Bill Bryce or one of the other neighbors, went out with their guns through one of the small woods or marshes whenever the snow was good for tracking. They hardly ever came back empty-handed. Kate liked the taste of fried wild rabbit. But Ivan had to skin and clean them. She declared that learning to clean a fresh-killed chicken was enough for the first year.

By Thanksgiving the ground was frozen solid and the lake had a thin coat of ice. Kate had looked forward to the lake freezing over so they could go ice skating. But now she knew she'd have to give it up for this winter. She was clumsy enough on her feet without adding a pair of skates.

They took a walk back to the lake one Sunday afternoon, and Kate marveled at the changed beauty there. The trees, now bare, made a picturesque silhouette against the snow covered lake. The black fields of muck were now white, only a few points of black showing here and there through the blanket, as though sleeping to ready themselves for the coming busy summer.

Kate and Ivan were invited to the Clodfelters for Thanksgiving dinner. It was a bountiful turkey dinner and good. Kate contributed her chocolate cake and again won compliments. Ivan took Helga the box with the little doll and shoes which Kate had found. Helga was pleased to have them. If there were still any hard feelings over the marble table, they weren't apparent.

It was at Christmas time that Kate met Ivan's brother, Claud. Claud and his wife Betty came Christmas Eve, spent Christmas Day and went back to Toledo the following day. Helga and family were also invited so they all could be together again on the farm for Christmas. But they had already invited Harry's family for the holiday.

Ivan's brother was not at all like Ivan, dark where Ivan was blond, and taller. He was good-humored and talkative, obviously devoted to his pretty wife. Betty was a good manager and good for Claud, Ivan told Kate later. He was doing far better in town with a job and a regular pay check than if he had stayed on a farm. Ivan tried not to be envious of him.

Kate was thrilled with every bit of the Christmas season and tried to start traditions between them that would last through the years with their children. The tree had to be in the bay window, temporarily replacing the marble table. It had to have one very special ornament marking their first Christmas; they would get a new one each year. She had creamed codfish for Christmas Eve supper, declaring that it was as close as she could come to a Norwegian dish in searching through her cookbook.

Ivan's gift to Kate was a picnic table and benches which he had made to set by the lake. He presented it to her by way of a note in a jewelry box placed under the tree. She had to go to the barn to find it and was completely thrilled. Her gift to him was a plaid wool cap with ear warmers and a pair of fur-lined gloves. Kraft company, where they sold their milk, gave the usual large box of caramels.

Several gifts from her parents arrived, along with sprigs of holly and Oregon walnuts from their own trees. A package came from Tommy and May Bell, obviously wrapped and mailed from a department store – a box of cheeses.

Kate continued to write to Tommy and May Bell, urging them to visit as soon as they could manage the trip. Letters from Kate's mother seldom mentioned the new daughter-in-law and Kate felt very apprehensive about the situation whenever she allowed herself to think about it. Was it a very close family pushing an outsider out? They had accepted Ivan. Or was it May Bell pulling the family apart?

January came and Kate marked off another month. Three more to go till time for the baby. On the colder days, they lived mostly in the kitchen where it was warm and cheerful. Although the winter weather was an inconvenience, Kate was not yet over being delighted with the snow. It blew and drifted as it never had back home. When there was snow during the winter in Portland, it merely sifted down and settled without packing and was often gone before the day was over. But here the snow was packed and crunchy underfoot. She'd noticed the difference during her winters at school and in Chicago, but here there was the wide expanse of it.

Ivan was helping Rocky build a two-wheel trailer on afternoons when there wasn't much else to do. Sometimes Kate went along and they both stayed till chore time.

"Spending an afternoon at the Rockwells is about like being at a restaurant," Kate sighed over the supper she wasn't hungry enough to eat, following one such day. "All that food around, and company coming day and night, I think Serena would get tired of that extra cooking and dishwashing."

"If she does, she never shows it," Ivan broke crackers into his bowl of chicken noodle soup. "It's the kind of life Rocky loves."

Kate got Michelle's version of that lifestyle a few afternoons later when she knocked on their door one Saturday looking unusually pale and solemn. With small talk Kate tried to find the problem, but it wasn't until she suggested she make them some cocoa that the confession came out.

"Please don't go to that bother," Shelly said and after a pause burst out close to tears, "I'm so sick of food, food, food all the time at home and a house full of company when I come home from school . . . and a kitchen full of dishes to do. Sometimes I just feel like running away."

Kate was shocked, but didn't reveal it. What could she say? "When you feel like running away be sure and come down here. I'm always so glad to have you come."

"I think Daddy must go out on the highway and stop the cars to find all the people he brings in for something to eat."

Kate smiled, nodding her sympathy and went on hemming baby diapers. Shelly was slumped on a chair at the table. "In the summer I can go to the hay loft in the barn or to my hideout in your woods, but now it's too cold. If only I had a little room of my own. Just any old cubbyhole with heat in it. But Daddy thinks that's a crazy idea. He says bedrooms are for sleeping not to sit around in."

Kate wondered why in that big house, Shelly couldn't have a comfortable room of her own, but said, "I guess every girl wants a room of her own. At least I would have been pretty unhappy without one."

"Your house is always so . . . so peaceful and nice."

"Then you come down just any time you want to and can. Bring a book along, or whatever you like. If you don't want to talk, I'll just go on with my work. I love to have you here."

So Shelly came more regularly for an hour or so in the afternoons, after school or on Saturdays, bringing a book. Often she'd bring a sweater and sit in the living room where it was not so warm as the kitchen, and sometimes she would bring bits of poetry to share with Kate. Kate was reminded of her brother who used to read poetry to the family. Was he reading those treasures to May Bell now?

Late in January there was a blizzard during below-zero weather. It snowed, blew, and drifted all one night and day. Kate and Ivan couldn't keep even the kitchen warm with the fires going constantly. The big square heating stove in the living room consumed log after log, but the big dining room drew out most of the heat. During the day, the bedroom door was kept shut. And as Kate sat shivering in their decorated privy, she was more determined than ever to have a bathroom before another winter.

Ivan was busy almost all day with chores. The stock had to be kept in fresh bedding, even though he let them out when the weather permitted. The ice had to be broken in the tank so they could drink. He added warm water to the chicken waterer when it was frozen. He fed the pigs warm slop prepared with hot water from the teakettle. Often the pump had to be thawed also from water heating on the cookstove. It was necessary to watch the brood sows frequently so one wouldn't farrow unexpectedly and the little pigs freeze before he found them.

But in spite of the constant battle against the weather, they had long evenings of fun, too, popping corn and eating apples from the cellar, playing cards, listening to the radio or reading. Sometimes they invited in a neighbor couple for the evening or a Sunday afternoon when the lane was passable with a car.

One clear cold day, when they were sure all the side roads had been plowed out, Kate and Ivan decided to go into Richland, sell their eggs, get groceries and do some other errands. "Let's take Mattie," Kate suggested. "I'll bet she hasn't been away from that house for weeks." They knew the Rockwells watched out for her during the cold weather since they were closer, but doubted if they took her into town unless she asked to go.

"Call her and see if she wants to go."

Mattie hesitated only a second before accepting. "Yes, I would like to git a few things in town t'day."

"We'll be by in about an hour." Kate wanted to be sure she understood Ivan would be going also.

While they were stopped in front of Mattie' s house and waiting for her to appear, Kate noticed the homely beauty of her weather beaten cottage. The sun shone on the deep drifts around it and the evergreen trees hung heavy with white. She hadn't seen Mattie since early Christmas Eve when she had stopped in, with Ivan waiting in the car, to leave her a Christmas gift of warm wool stockings and a box of homemade candy. Mattie had been touched by the presents and said she was having Christmas dinner with the Rockwells.

She crept carefully down the path which she had so laboriously shoveled and to the waiting car. Kate opened the door for her and scooted over toward Ivan. "Ain't sech a bad day," Mattie said without any other greeting. And they were off to town through the narrow country road between the high, sharp banks of snow.

After they had parked in town, Kate told Mattie to do her shopping or whatever else she wanted to do and come back to the car when she was through. "Don't hurry now and fall on the icy spots," Kate warned. "We've lots of time."

When Ivan and Kate returned, they found Mattie already waiting in the car, her few parcels and groceries in the black oilcloth bag. When they drove up again in front of the Enders' house she turned to them. "S'pose you wouldn't come in fer a cup of cocoa an' a piece o' gingerbread? I jest got through baking some."

Kate looked at Ivan. He smiled. "It's been a long time since I tasted Aunt Mattie's gingerbread."

As they entered the warm kitchen, Ivan looked around with interest. "Your kitchen sure looks familiar, but for some reason it seems smaller than it used to."

"I guess you growed some since then." She went about making the cocoa. "Ivan, would you poke up thet fire and add to it? Kate, there's some cups in thet cupboard there, some little plates t'match."

Soon they were seated at the table, biting into big squares of sorghum molasses gingerbread and sipping hot cocoa. Mattie said to Ivan, "You ain't changed a bit, only bigger. Where's thet brother an' sister of yers?"

Ivan briefly told about them. He tried to tell how he'd taken over the place but skirted around any mention of his parents, either before or after their accident.

"What about thet ol' dinner bell in yer wood shed? I ain't heard it in years. A body used to hear it about ever day, yer ma callin' em in to dinner 'n all."

"Oh, it's still there, but tied up high out of the reach of kids wanting to ring it."

Kate looked astonished. "I didn't even know there was such a thing in the wood shed. I'm going to look as soon as I get home."

"A body could hear it all over these parts and if it rang morn' once, it meant trouble."

"Yeah, Mom always said she felt safe with that bell to ring if she needed help."

They leisurely finished their refreshments and Kate helped gather up the dishes. She thanked Mattie, then turned to leave, but saw Ivan hesitate and turn back. He held out his hand, "Aunt Mattie, I just want you to know that if I'm still around when your time comes, yours will be as nice as any funeral ever held in our church."

She covered his hand with both of hers, bowed her head to hide her eyes and said, "Bless you, my boy, bless you, bless you . . ."

CHAPTER 21

Easter 1936

KATE WAS EXTREMELY TIRED of winter and yearned for spring. Fresh snow no longer thrilled her. She wanted to see green grass and the first robin instead. And time for the baby dragged on so slowly. It was no joke to her that she was as wide as she was tall.

The ice house was filled for another summer's supply. Filling it was an experience similar to filling the silo. There was the dinner to get, but this time for only a few of their closest neighbors, those who would be using the ice. Ivan said his mother always had steamed brown bread (the recipe was marked "steamed cornbread") and baked beans for the ice house gang and Kate thought it a good idea.

Another community practice which Kate found interesting was the farm auctions. If a farm family were moving and needed to raise money, or for some other reason wanted to dispose of all or part of their possessions, they held an auction sale, advertising it widely. As a result, some people came from a considerable distance and stayed all day. If it was a large sale, an aid society from a local church served hot lunch. The pre-spring months was the time for farm auctions, before farmers got busy with the spring field work. March was traditionally moving month. The sale Kate went to with Ivan reminded her of a little carnival or fair and she was excited over the bargains she'd bid off. Ivan had to go back next day with Rocky's pickup truck to bring home what he laughingly called "all her junk."

"But just imagine that cute little rocker for fifty cents! And that chest of drawers is good hard wood; won't I have fun refinishing them?" But Kate realized she was over tired from standing so long and jostling with the crowd. She'd have to wait till after the baby was born to attend any more auctions.

In the early evenings after they'd eaten supper and before Kate tumbled wearily into bed, the two Andersons sat over the kitchen table with seed catalogs, magazines, text books and a large white sheet of drawing paper on which Ivan had drawn the whole farm to scale. He moved crops from one field to another until the plan for the following year was as good as he could make it. He wanted to go in for potatoes, peppermint, or some other muck crop, but finally decided that it was too much of a gamble for them just yet. It would mean more machinery and seeking new markets. Eventually he wanted cash crops second in importance to dairying anyway. So he'd do what he could with the onions until a good-producing dairy herd was built up and he had a milk house and other facilities to qualify for grade A milk. There was the need for more high ground to grow feed.

Kate remembered her menu planning on paper and admired his paper farm. Actually she was much interested in the diagram too, especially in plans around the buildings. She sketched in each shrub, tree and clump of flowers that grew around the house, then together they moved them at liberty. It made Kate all the more eager for the snow to leave and spring to come, so they could get started on their project.

But there were several weeks of bad weather yet. Ivan could see her restlessness and waning interest in sewing, refinishing furniture and the other things that had kept her busy and happy. He wanted to help her find a new interest and stumbled on it quite by chance.

He'd fallen on the slippery thawing snow and had broken a handful of eggs he was carrying. "Ten or fifteen years ago that would have been a major catastrophe about this time of year," he remembered. "When we were kids, we used to hide eggs ten days before Easter. Any of us could pick them up and take them to a hiding place any time of day – if we were lucky enough not to be seen by the others."

"And what happened if you got caught?"

"Then that person knew his hiding place and could secretly steal his eggs. The loser would have to start over. On Easter morning all the eggs were brought in and counted and the winner's reward was to market all the eggs and keep the money."

"Oh, what fun! Something else Tommy and I missed by not living on a farm."

"Dad usually talked us into buying something the others could use, too. That's how we got our first bicycle. We had more hens than we've got now."

"Let's do it this year. Just you and I," Kate urged.

"I'd beat you a mile. Don't you realize I know every hiding place on this farm?"

"You just think you do. I know lots of places you'd never think to look."

Ivan grudgingly agreed. "But don't you go running around in the slush and fall, breaking more than the eggs."

"Yes, Grandma, I'll be careful." She patted his cheek.

"No running to Mattie Enders, either. They have to be kept on the farm and someplace they won't freeze when a real cold night comes along, or spoil from being too warm."

So the egg-hiding began. Ivan entered into it only enough to let her know she'd have to keep at it to beat him. He made a pretense of searching for her eggs, always afraid he would find them.

Due date for the baby was April 15; Easter was April 12. Never-the-less Kate insisted she was going to fix an Easter dinner just for the two of them, since she had been sick on the day of their recent wedding anniversary.

After supper on Easter Eve, Kate still had the cake to put together. It was a white cake and as she explained to Ivan at supper, she was going to cover it with fluffy white frosting and whole hickory nuts. "Just like the picture in my cookbook."

Ivan usually cracked the hard-shelled little nuts for her, using a hammer to break them on an old flat iron turned upside down between his knees. But tonight he didn't see any waiting on the back porch, so when he came in with the last of the milk, he picked up an old pan, and went to the cellar after them.

There were four lard cans lined up side by side on the wooden shelf along the wall. One of them should contain the nuts. The first of the 20-pound lard cans felt empty, the next one had lard in it, the next, with the lid ajar . . . eggs! Kate's Easter eggs. Almost full to the top. He closed the lid quickly and opened the last can, which did have nuts in it.

Suddenly he heard Kate shout, "Are you getting the nuts? They're in the end can to the right!"

He didn't answer, knowing his voice would betray him. Then he heard her hurrying heavily toward the cellar door. "Did you hear me?" she shouted again. "They're in the end can to the right."

"No, I can't hear you, I haven't got my ear phone with me," he called back, daring to laugh now as he noisily raked up hickory nuts and dropped them into the pan. "Who do you think put these nuts in a can and carried them down here anyway?"

She looked suspiciously at him when he came up, but his face revealed nothing. Where in the dickens had she found all those eggs!?! She must have bought or borrowed some.

An hour later, Kate was adding the last of the whole nuts to the top of the cake, so tired she wanted nothing but to climb into bed. A dull pain centered in her lower back made her sink into a chair and utter, "Oh-h."

"Do you suppose this is it?" she said with rising excitement.

Ivan was immediately full of solicitude and wanted to hurry her right to the hospital.

Kate shook her head. "No chance of it coming that fast. The doctor said the first baby might take as long as eighteen hours. But I'll show him. Anyway I hope it waits till midnight. An Easter baby, think of that!"

By nine o'clock she was sure of being in labor though the pains were irregular and not severe. The tiredness forgotten, she was thinking only that the long, long wait would soon be over. They would know whether it was boy or girl, how big and what it looked like. There was little fear of the ordeal ahead of her.

She finished packing her overnight case and again checked the little nursery off their bedroom with its ivy wallpaper and pastel green sateen-lined basket. Occasionally she took time to sit out a pain, or fire orders at Ivan, who was hurriedly and nervously washing the rest of the dishes. "Don't forget to water the plants . . . send a telegram to Mother and Dad right away . . . eat regular meals, now, don't just snack. There's that ham on the back porch, you know. And you ought to have cake to last for awhile." She laughed overloud in her excitement.

She stopped short. "Our Easter eggs! I won't be here in the morning. Let's bring them in now."

"Are you sure we've got time?" He wished she hadn't thought of them.

"Yes, of course, the pains have sort of gone away."

"All right, where do I go to get yours?" He hurriedly put the dishpan away.

"You get yours first."

Ivan picked up a pail from the porch and hurried toward the barn. He didn't want to leave her long. He opened the lid to the grain drill and picked up the sack. There was nothing. How in the devil . . .? He'd added two more at four o'clock when he found them in one of the old horse stalls. She must have taken them while he was milking. No wonder that lard can was full! He returned to the house sheepishly carrying an empty pail. Kate was sitting at the kitchen table merrily laughing. "Who was it going to beat me a mile?"

"How long have you known where they were?"

"That's my secret. Now when I tell you where mine are, you'll know how close you came to finding them tonight. They're down in the cellar in a lard can next to the nuts." She got up and hugged him, the physical breach between them considerable now.

They stood together laughing in the middle of the kitchen floor until another pain overtook Kate and she sat down again.

After they were at the Richland Memorial Hospital and Kate had been prepped for delivery, she lay in bed, Ivan by her side, as the contractions began to get more severe. Through them she winced, panted and tossed, but between pains she was talkative and still bubbling with joy. Somewhere someone was going through this every hour of every day. Now it was her turn. It wouldn't last long, she was sure. But the minutes grew into hours and the hours added up, and still the nurse said there was little progress.

She kept asking Ivan what time it was, as he sat, walked around the room, or bent over her, looking pale and anxious. At day break he went to the window and pointed out the streaks of daylight across the eastern sky above the sleeping town – Easter morning.

By the time Kate heard the breakfast trays being carried down the hall, she could no longer be cheerful. She was so very, very tired and the pains left her no time to rest. She'd just drop off to sleep when another one started. The night nurse had gone off duty and another came on, a pleasant woman, but also very busy with several new mothers and babies to attend.

Ivan had given up hope of getting home to his chores and called Bill Bryce about them. Kate urged him to go out and get some breakfast even though the night nurse had brought him coffee. "You're waiting on a woman this time instead of a cow or a sow." She smiled wanly with a last attempt at cheer.

"Anyway, it isn't quite so cold in here as it is in the barn."

The doctor came, examined her, told her it would still be awhile and not to get discouraged, then talked to Ivan out in the hall and left. Not be discouraged! With babies crying in the nursery whose mothers had come in after she did? People going to church in their new spring outfits and she was in a crazy old night shirt turned backwards, her hair tangled and matted. She wanted to scream for more attention from the busy nurse. Women going through this every hour of every day for centuries . . . oh, Lord, why?

Her mind between the pains, was a hazy blur from weariness and the sedation. Familiar voices, strange voices, came to her without shape or form of human body – giving orders, encouragement, sympathy. Only part of it reached her, then the voices would float away again. She wept and moaned. I can't take any more. The next pain will split me wide open like that old apple tree in the orchard the day the lightning struck it, and I'm going to scream . . . but she didn't.

Her eyes opened briefly and she realized she was under the bright lights of the delivery room. White-clad people were working over her with penetrating smells and tinny voices. Someone was rubbing the insides of her thighs with what felt like ice. She was already frozen. Her arms and legs were caught; she couldn't move. Another pain was beginning; she opened her mouth to scream. But a smothering mask was held over her nose and mouth, stopping it. A calm voice commanded, "Breath deeply, Mrs. Anderson, breathe deeply."

Kate gulped obediently to win the race with pain and hoped this was the last. But it wasn't. Again and again she came to long enough to be told to bear down with the beginning of the pain, then quickly breathe the anesthetic. Finally she shook her head in protest. I can't. Someone else will have to take over.

Then the deep, kindly voice of Dr. Carter penetrated through to her, "Don't give up now, Kate . . . you've been a brave girl . . . baby almost here . . . once more."

All right. Might as well go on in this blue vacuum of departed spirits, stupidly grunting away the constant torture. She gathered strength for one hard push and was gone again.

She was conscious once more and expected to be told to repeat the same process. But no pain came. She tried to lift her heavy arms and found them free. She sensed a peace and quiet about her. Was this Heaven? She managed to place a hand on her stomach. It was flat, empty and bound. Then she was aware of being in a fresh bed, warm and comfortable. Her eyes fluttered opened at the slight movement beside her and she recognized Ivan bending over her.

"What . . . is . . . it?"

"Our little boy, honey. All eight and one-half pounds of him."

A boy. Edward Ivan Anderson. Eddie.

Then Ivan laid his cheek against hers. "Oh, Katy, my darling, what you've been through!"

She drifted off to sleep again for a few minutes. "Is it still Easter?"

"For three whole hours, yet."

"Have you been home to your chores?"

"No. Bill did them again."

Good old Bill. Poor Ida. Poor anyone . . . who never knew the pride of accomplishment to push one's way through hell to find Heaven waiting on the other side – with a little baby boy.

"Go home now, darling." She lifted her heavy hand to his cheek and tried to see him. "You must be tired to death. I can sleep for ten days straight, but you can't."

"Yes, I am tired, and hungry. I'll go home and send that telegram to your mother and dad. Then I'm going to eat some ham and some of that cake. Maybe all of it at once." He kissed her tenderly and saw that she was asleep before he left the room.

The next morning Kate was still very weak and tired, but supremely happy. By early afternoon Ivan had returned. He was beaming and Kate thought it was the new-father look. But there was other news. "I stopped by this morning and told Mattie about the baby."

"Oh, I'm so glad you did."

"She was tickled and insisted I stay for dinner."

"Really!"

"And before we were through eating, here she was asking me to take over her place this spring."

"Bless her dear old soul. What did you say?"

"I was so surprised, I didn't know what to tell her right off. Then she said that kid she had last year didn't amount to a 'hill o' beans.' She went on to say she could trust me now." Kate smiled and nodded. "So she said if I had 'a mind to' to come up some day and we'd talk it over. Of course she added, 'But I'm not too old to keep a finger on things. I know more about farmin' than most people think.' " Ivan ended the tale laughing. "I guess she's a good old egg after all." He suddenly jumped up. "I almost forgot something I brought for you. I'll be right back."

Kate was expecting a box of candy, that she'd have to try to keep from eating now that it was time to lose weight. But he returned carrying something heavy in a cloth sugar sack. Whatever was it?

He laid the bag at her side and she looked in. Pennys. Hundreds of them. "I sold your Easter eggs."

She swatted him with the back of her hand. "I was going to buy something you could enjoy, too, but now I'll just save them for Eddie."

"I got the idea from great grandfather Andrew. He brought great grandma a bag of coins when he sold their New York farm."

"Except that was two hundred dollars!" They laughed together and squeezed hands. "Did you see the baby today?" Kate asked.

"Yes, on the way in."

"Kind of red for an Easter lily, isn't he?"

"Better not insult him too much; he looks just like you," Ivan grinned.

"He doesn't either. He looks like you."

"I've got hair, he hasn't."

They kissed and wished they were home. The three of them.

CHAPTER 22

The Bell Tolls

AFTER TEN DAYS, Kate and Eddie came home from the hospital. She was weak, but with Ivan's help, managed to get the necessary work done. Serena sent food and Shelly offered to help when she was needed. On Kate's birthday, Eddie was just two weeks old. Ivan asked her how she wanted to celebrate.

"Let's go to the Sweet Shop when we go in to get groceries after dinner," she said eagerly, "and I'll get to wear one of my pre-maternity dresses. It's a nice day out. We'll wrap up Eddie and take him for his first outing. Then we can sit in the car while you buy the groceries."

So baby Eddie had his first trip to the Sweet Shop, where he slept on the table beside them while they ate their chocolate sundaes covered with peanuts.

Then Kate and the baby sat in the car while Ivan went to the Kroger store. Two farmers stood talking by the car next to Kate. She gathered they were discussing the prison break which had been on the front page for the last couple of days. Polosky, a criminal involved in a series of bank robberies, had escaped from the state penitentiary in Pendleton. Kate's busy days since she came home from the hospital did not include reading the paper, but she had noticed the headlines and read the captions under the pictures.

"I heard this morning, they think he might be headed in this direction. He's got a relative over around Onion Center someplace," said the man in striped overalls.

The other man commented, "The state police probably's got a stake out around the house. They'll get him."

"Well, anyway I'm not going to pick up any hitchhikers on my way home." They laughed and separated.

Kate shuddered and thought of Mattie Enders. Her little dark house almost hidden by pine trees would be a likely target for a fugitive like that.

Right along the highway, too. On the other hand, Mattie and her twenty-two might be a match for just about any man, Kate chuckled.

They didn't discuss the news on the way home. Ivan had gotten some early garden seed and they eagerly planned their garden for the year.

Ivan would get the garden plowed and help her plant peas, lettuce and radishes. Then by the time they were up and growing, Kate felt she would be ready to take over. She loved gardening.

"And this year Eddie can go with us to bring in the produce from the muck garden." She snuggled the baby to her. "We'll just prop you up in an onion crate even though you won't be ready to eat a turnip yet."

After Ivan got his family in the house and settled, he had to hurry to Bill Bryce's to do his chores before starting his own. Bill and Ida were visiting relatives in Ohio overnight. The ground was still too wet to plow, so both men had spare time.

Kate left the groceries on the kitchen table where Ivan had set them so she could nurse the baby. He hadn't eaten for three hours and was just beginning to let her know about it.

She nursed him for about ten minutes when there was a loud knocking at the back door, so loud it startled both her and the baby just as he was drifting back to sleep. Whoever it was had come across the back porch and to the kitchen door. Had there been a car accident? Or was someone in trouble back at the lake and needed help? Neighbors usually just called in to them. She quickly laid the baby in his basket, pulled up her brassier and buttoned her dress, then hurried toward the kitchen. As she approached the dining room door that opened into the kitchen, she was stunned into complete horror. A man was entering the kitchen with a gun pointed at her. She knew immediately it matched the gaunt, arrogant face on the front page of the morning's paper. She leaned against the door jamb for support as fear raced through her body, her head throbbing, her heart pounding.

"Are you alone?" he demanded sourly.

What should she say? That Ivan was at the barn or that Rockwells were nearby? No. She must demonstrate absolute obedience. Try to win his confidence. "I'm . . . alone," she gasped.

"Then get me men's clothes and food. QUICK!"

"Just . . . a . . . minute. I'm afraid if I move I'll faint."

"MOVE!" He flicked the gun. The sudden command sent the blood surging to her head. She expected the gun to go off any second. Anguish enveloped her. My baby . . . Ivan.

"I'll . . . get . . . clothes . . . from . . . my . . . husband's dresser." She walked awkwardly back toward the bedroom aware that he followed for a few steps but remained in the kitchen. He must have been close by and watched Ivan leave.

Once inside the bedroom she had a fleeting thought to slam the door – which didn't even have a lock – or grab Eddie and get out a window. But that would mean their certain end. No. She must get the clothes and return.

She opened Ivan's drawer of work clothes, took out a blue shirt and overalls, then, not knowing for sure that was what he wanted, she opened the closet door and, rattling the hangers, took down Ivan's best suit. She took a last glance at Eddie asleep in the basket. "Oh, dear God, don't let him waken and cry." Then she forced her steps back to the kitchen. The desperado still held the gun steady, but now not so directly at her. She felt a bit of relief. Now if nothing from outside disturbed him. She held the clothes out to him. In his free hand he took the suit on the hanger, glanced at it, and threw it against the wall.

"Roll them up!" He indicated the work clothes. "Put 'em in that big sack with some food. Bread, meat, whatever you got. Fast!" He pointed with the gun to the grocery sack.

She quickly spilled out the contents, trying not to make too much noise. Oranges rolled off the table onto the floor. He snatched up a couple and put them in the pocket of his muddy penitentiary-issued coveralls. Kate jerked off the string from a package of meat to be sure it was the wieners and seeing that it was, dumped them into the sack, shakily hurrying as fast as she could.

"There's cold meat, beans and a loaf of bread." As she was rolling up the top of the sack, there was a loud clang. A new frenzy of fear seized her. But he had grabbed the bag, swung around and was creeping toward the door – gun ready.

Suddenly it occurred to Kate it had been the sound of the old dinner bell. One gong. She'd lived here for a year and had never heard it. Whoever rang it was in extreme danger. She held her breath as she saw the felon slide out the door, edge along the back of the house away from the sound of the bell and dart toward the woods.

Overcome with weakness, Kate wanted to sink into a chair, but she must hold out a little longer. She went to the telephone and rang a wild, short ring. The sound echoed through the house.

Breathlessly she told the operator, "Get me the state police in Richland . . . quickly." In a matter of seconds a deep efficient voice answered.

"Polosky . . . has . . . been . . . here. He came for . . . food and clothes. Was frightened off into the woods."

"Who is this? Where are you?" The voice demanded quickly, but kindly.

"Do you know the old Stangland farm . . near Onion Center?"

A pause, then she heard him turn from the phone and say: "Polosky!"

"Which way from Onion Center?"

"East – no west. Rockwells?"

"Earnie Rockwell? Yes! Where from there?"

"South . . . down a lane from their place," she panted with shaking voice. He asked her to repeat and she realized she was hardly speaking above a whisper.

"We'll be there in a few minutes. Stay inside and out of sight." Kate replaced the receiver with a weak and shaking hand. Suddenly she realized that whoever was in the woodshed with the bell hadn't come in yet. It couldn't have been Ivan. She saw no one before or after the bell rang. Michelle had come every afternoon since the baby came. But how could she have gotten to the woodshed unseen? Kate slipped out the front door around the edge of the porch and entered the old woodshed. In the darkened interior she saw only the bell hanging high out of reach. Had it tolled by itself? Then her eyes fell on a crumbled heap of calico on the dirty floor among the wood chips. She recognized the dress and bonnet of Mattie Enders.

Kate dropped to her knees. "Oh, no, no! Mattie! Mattie!" She felt in her neck for a pulse, but there was none. Apparently she had noiselessly climbed up on the cord of wood to reach and pull the bell rope as her heart beat its last.

With difficulty, Kate rose and moved back towards the house and fell into the arms of Serena Rockwell, just approaching on the run. Kate sobbed out the story to her capable neighbor and let herself be led into the house, where she was made comfortable on the bed beside the still sleeping Eddie in his basket. Then Serena went to the telephone to call the doctor as the state police roared down the lane. They instructed Mrs. Rockwell to notify the telephone operator to ring a long ring on each line in the neighborhood, always a signal of utmost importance, to notify each family to stay in their homes with doors locked until further notified.

In a matter of an hour the fugitive was captured and taken out of the Anderson woods. Mattie's body was taken away. But Kate heard or saw little of it. She was in a deep sleep from sedation administered by Dr. Carter.

Ivan returned just as the police cars were leaving and was met in the driveway by newsmen and photographers. His face drained of all color, he leaped from the car. "Wha . . . what's happened?"

"They've taken that fugitive, Polosky, from a thicket by the lake," said the editor of the *Richland Weekly*.

"My wife . . . my baby!"

"They're all right, but they won't let us talk to her. Get what facts you can and bring them out to us. Will you, Ive?"

After Ivan had turned away the newsmen, he hovered over the sleeping Kate and his two-week-old son, realizing how precious they were to him. And how grateful he was to God and Aunt Mattie Enders who had watched over them.

As for Kate's birthday – it was one to be remembered.

CHAPTER 23

Letters

TRUE TO HIS WORD, Ivan went to Earnie Rockwell's the next morning to see about arrangements for Mattie Enders' funeral and he found him at the hog house mixing pig feed.

"You must have made a mighty big impression on the poor old soul. Or maybe was your wife did it." Rocky said when they began discussing events of the day before. "We opened her envelope last night. She's given us different ones through the years, kind of like a will, I guess. As she changed her mind, she brought a new sealed envelope and took away the old. I'm sure what she says will stand up in court since it's in her hand writing and no one to contest it that I know of." He stopped long enough to pour slop in the trough behind him to quiet the pigs, then turned back with a broad smile. "Looks like you've inherited yourself a farm, Ive. You and that peace-making wife of yours."

Ivan flushed, momentarily stunned. "Do you mean she left her farm to *me*!?!"

"That's right."

"After all the hard feelings and the things *you* folks have done for her?"

Rocky pushed back his hat and leaned on the side of the pen. "Oh, I'm sure that in one of those letters it was willed to us. I was afraid of it when I opened this one. It would have been a headache to me, Ive, that odd shaped piece across the road. I would have had to tear down most of the buildings and look out for an empty house. I wouldn't feel right selling it, but it would be a white elephant on my hands. It adjoins your property, though. Might do you some good, if you got time to work over those buildings."

"I'm flabergasted to say the least. Sure, I can use it, even if the buildings have to sit awhile. It's all high ground, what I need to build up my dairying." He looked at Rocky a moment, then asked, "Did you know about the trouble?"

"Yes-s. Certainly was a tempest in a teapot. That preacher left just before we bought our farm. He must have been a lemon for sure."

"She told Kate he kept going out there trying to . . . make it with Mattie."

"Is that right! No wonder she was so bitter. What an abomination for the church. Although I suppose no one knew it but her. Poor old girl. Well, that's water under the bridge. Now we got to see about that funeral she says you're going to give her."

"She even mentioned it in the letter, did she? Yes, I promised her that last winter."

"When I saw you folks going there quite a little bit, I knew some things must be getting straightened out. Rena and me, we were just tickled to death."

"Give Kate all the credit. She couldn't rest until the Andersons and Mattie Enders were on good terms again."

The two men went into the house to go over Mattie's instructions together. The two sisters in Missouri, whose addresses she gave, were to be notified. A head stone matching Robert's was to be erected from any available funds. "She may have money stuck away in that house somewhere," Rocky suspected.

"I ought to be able to afford a pretty fine stone for a whole farm. And I'm sure Kate will see that those graves are never neglected."

Ivan was anxious to get back to his wife with the news; but first he must visit Pastor Sorenson concerning the funeral. For a moment though, as he shook hands with Earnie Rockwell, Ivan admired the man in front of him. Earnest Rockwell knew the difference between contentment and greed. Pure gold was this rock of a man.

When Ivan came home at noon, Kate could tell that he hadn't just been planning a funeral. She heard the news with awe, then tears. After the impact of yesterday, she was still highly emotional. "Mattie, dear Mattie," she cried against Ivan. "All morning I've felt so close to her. She's with her Robert and Rowland at last. And she'll be laid out there in the peaceful cemetery that she loved so much – under the pine trees beside Robert. And, Ivan, look what I found." She picked up a small waxpaper-wrapped package of gingerbread from the cabinet. "It was by the gate post where she must have slipped through unnoticed when she saw Polosky coming to the door. I'm sure she was bringing it for my birthday."

It was not a large funeral, but beautiful with flowers which Kate had selected from the florists and added early crocus from Mattie's yard and garden. The minister's message centered around her quiet life and love of flowers. He emphasized her unassuming service to the church through her music and her work at the cemetery.

Michelle Rockwell came down to keep little Eddie while Kate and Ivan attended. She already adored the baby. Once when she was visiting, Kate overheard her singing a quiet little lullaby as she rocked him.

The day after the funeral, Mr. Brown from the funeral home called and asked if it was the home of a "Kate?" He said there was an envelope addressed to her in the apron pocket of the clothes Mattie wore and asked if they would like to pick it up along with the clothes. Kate knew Serena had gone into Mattie's house and got the black silk dress for burial as Mattie had instructed in the envelope given to Rockwells.

Ivan drove in after the clothes and the letter and handed the package to Kate. She unwrapped the bundle slowly and reverently. The envelope addressed to her lay on top of the neatly folded garments. It was quite bulky. "She must have included a handkerchief or doily along with the birthday card," Kate reasoned. She turned the envelope over and over, thinking of Mattie. Then slowly opened it, unfolded the sheet of yellow tablet paper to reveal a sheaf of bills . . . one hundred dollar bills!

Kate held them helplessly for a moment, then began reading from the Note: "Dear little nabor I am riting this because I don't think I can tell you to yer face how much you have ment to me this past year . . ." Tears were blinding Kate; she could no longer see nor speak and handed the letter to Ivan. He continued: "This is the money from Robert's fund, witch I was savin for lectricity when it coms. He was always so intrested in that but now I know I don't want to make any changes sense I can go to town and the semetary whenever I want. I like things jest as they is. It is my greatest plasure for you to have your bathroom fer all them ice creams and trips you took me and yer settin and a listin to me and all. Happy Birthday yer friend Mattie."

Part Two

CHAPTER 24

Tommy's Story

THE LATE AFTERNOON SUN shone warm on the tulips, red and white, lining the side of the old woodshed. Over the cookie-making, Kate smiled out the window at two-year-old Eddie playing in the sandbox. He had been so good all day when she was extra busy. His baby sister, Nancy – Nan – seven months old, was sleeping. At least there was a bathroom for that pregnancy and a much easier delivery.

Electricity had come through also, but they could only afford the wiring, lights, an electric pump for water and a motor on their old Thor washing machine. At least the wedding presents needing electricity could now be used. She reveled in the shiny electric iron. And a mixer now made her near-famous chocolate cakes. The stove and refrigerator would have to come later. She hoped it would be before hot weather.

Kate sighed. She would enjoy being outdoors, working in her flowers or planting garden. But she mustn't give in to that temptation with Tommy arriving tomorrow.

It had been three years since Kate had seen her brother. To think that, as close as they were all the years growing up and through college, so much time could separate them now. She knew that financially it would have been possible for him and May Bell to come for a visit during one of his vacations, but the reason they hadn't come was – May Bell. He couldn't very well come without her, and she wouldn't waste those two weeks stuck on a farm in some out-of-the-way place in Indiana.

Kate's parents seldom mentioned May Bell in their letters. But during the trip to Indiana to visit their first grandchild (in the fall when Eddie was five months old), her mother could no longer keep from revealing her extreme dislike of the strange-acting daughter-in-law.

Now Tommy and May Bell were separated and she had custody of their baby girl. Although divorce was an ugly word in the Morgan family, all were relieved when it was the means by which May Bell White left the family for good. Tommy had written a short note to Kate saying that he was coming by for a good visit before beginning his new job in Pennsylvania. He would "lick his wounds" as he moved to a new region and get back "on the road," he wrote.

Kate put another stick of wood in the range and slid the last pan of cookies into the oven. She heard Eddie: "Daddy, Daddy – cake f' you." Then Ivan's voice joined his and she knew he had come to get the milk pails.

Tommy arrived late the next afternoon, his car well packed for his new life in Pennsylvania. He had driven in while both children were napping and Kate was taking down diapers from the line. He slipped around to the back of the house and called out, "Wanta' buy some books, lady?" She squealed and he hugged her and the armload of clothes. "Where's the brass band? A fine reception I get after three long years."

Ivan had just come in with the tractor and came to join them. The two men exchanged greetings and small talk, giving Kate an opportunity to stand aside and get over her shock of seeing the change in Tommy. He had aged much more than three years. There was obvious gray in his black hair, and fine lines around eyes that didn't twinkle and smile as they used to. He was thin, much too thin, making him appear tall and gaunt. Her heart cried out: May Bell, what have you done to him!?!

Tommy turned again to her. "Being a farmer's wife and a mother seems to agree with you. You haven't changed." Kate wished she could say the same to him, but instead took his arm and started toward the house. Tommy looked around. "You weren't kidding when you said this was a picture book farm. This is first rate! But where are the cows and the onions? I brought a brand new pair of Oshkosh B'Gosh overalls, Ive, and expect to break them in."

"Get into them, then. I'm about ready to milk."

"Didn't you bring cowboy boots and a ten-gallon hat?" Kate asked. "The Rockwell boys are expecting you to have them."

"That's a family I've got to meet. Say, I like this, too." He rubbed his hands over the gentle fire in the cookstove and with the iron hook he lifted one of the lids and peered inside. Kate watched him and tried to recapture some of the joy she felt when first she warmed herself over that stove three years ago. Now she would gladly replace its coziness for a shiny new efficient electric range.

The children were awake; Kate could hear them chattering. She went to their room and returned, leading Eddie and carrying Nan. Shyly burying his face in his mother's dress, Eddie said, "Oncle Tom-mee."

Tommy greeted them cordially, but not with the warmth Kate had expected. Did they only remind him of his own small daughter who had been taken from him?

That evening, after the dishes were done, the children in bed and Ivan off to a meeting of the Farm Bureau, of which he was president, Kate and Tommy had their first opportunity for a serious visit. She had wondered if the breach of years and events between them would end Tommy's confiding in her.

They sat in the living room reminiscing and talking of family until the children went to sleep. When all was quiet in the bedroom, Kate went to check on them, laid aside the teddy bear snuggled close to Eddie, straightened out and covered Nan. When she returned, Tommy was up and fidgeting about the room again as he seemed to be every free moment. Like a man recently freed from prison, Kate thought grimly, but she said only, "Well, the children are asleep for another night." She sat on the couch, slipped off her shoes and propped herself against the pillows.

Tommy finally returned to his chair and lit another cigarette. "Lucky, lucky you with two such lovely children."

Kate nodded a thank you. "I'd love to see Sheila."

"So would I," Tommy said bitterly, "So would I."

"You have joint custody, don't you?"

"On paper, yes, but that's all – unless I start suing and I don't want to do that." He sighed. "You know, after I moved out and I'd go back to take her for a ride or to Mom and Dad's or someplace, May Bell had Sheila so alienated from me, she'd cry and resist until it was too painful for me to carry through with it. Once I did entice her away and her mother sent along such a detailed schedule and so much paraphernalia, I didn't try again."

Kate shook her head sadly. "How old is she now?"

"Just a year and a half."

"Mom wrote that she's a beautiful child."

"That she is. Looks like her mother."

"I bet she's got some Morgan Irish spunk in her anyway."

"I hope so, because there is little I can do now except send her a present now and then, and hope May Bell will give it to her and explain where it came from. When she's older I can write directly to her and get acquainted." He paused in his misery and finally continued. "Kate, how could I have gotten myself and our family in such a mess? I hate it like the devil, but I don't know what to do about it . . . except stay out of town and let it die down as much as possible. Even so, May Bell is still there and with Morgan for a name. She's having the time of her life, playing the part of a deserted mother."

"I can imagine." Kate remembered her style. "Not many people are going to be fooled – those who matter most anyway. May Bell is pretty well known for what she is."

"How could I have misjudged her so completely?"

"Don't blame yourself so much, Tommy. She's a good actress and it's your nature to trust people. May Bell discovered that along with your irresistible charm and went to work. You know the folks used to say you were the romanticist and me – old Practical Pat."

"Yes. Katherine Patricia – Kate Pat – and look what you've got." He shook his head wretchedly. "Why didn't you warn me?"

"I should have, Tommy, I honestly should have, knowing May Bell as I did in high school. But I didn't think a man in love would listen any more than I would have if you'd warned me against marrying a farmer. Then, if your marriage did work out, as I sincerely hoped it would, there would be that wedge between us."

"Yes, I suppose you're right. I'm glad your marriage turned out so well anyway."

"I have a lot to be thankful for." Kate sighed. "Ivan has been a model husband and father. I still like this grand old house, but how I wish we had just a little more money to spend! We're poor, Tommy, down right poor. We have plenty of food; we raise our vegetables and butcher for meat. But there is so little for clothes and improving the house. In the three years we've been here, I bet I haven't spent on clothes for myself what I previously spent in one month." It seemed strange to be telling these intimate facts to Tommy, but she knew they would be safe with him. He wouldn't mention them to either Ivan or her parents.

"When I came to this place after we were married, I thought it was quaint and wonderful in spite of having neither electricity nor inside plumbing. We expected to have so many things after that first year. I wrote you, didn't I, about the windfall from Mattie Enders, an old neighbor lady?" He nodded. "Bless her heart. After that I shouldn't complain. When rural electrification came through we thought we'd have everything we wanted." She paused and sighed. "Boy, have I learned some things about farming since then! Ivan, too, I think. He was going to build up a full-blooded dairy herd and have a milking machine. But it was one expense after another. The children, of course, which we certainly don't regret. Then there was the expense of wiring for electricity. He hasn't had a good year for onions since we've been here. Drouth the first year, which doesn't effect muck ground so much, but it didn't *help* them either. They were small and the price was low. The second year it was a late spring and too wet. Then last year, there was a fairly decent crop, but expenses ate up the profit. There is a lot of hand labor in raising onions – weeding, pulling, topping and screening – and he has to pay more and more to get it done."

In spite of himself, Tommy suddenly laughed. "I'm sorry, I'm not laughing at your plight, but because I never dreamed I'd hear my city-bred sister tossing around the vernacular of an onion farmer."

Kate arched her eyebrows. "One learns when put to the challenge."

"I'm sorry it's been such a struggle, really I am."

"We should have taken dozens of pictures when we first came here to compare them with what the place looks like now. Then we could see what we've accomplished."

"The whole farm looks like something out of a book to me. But of course I'm not the one who has to cook on a wood range."

"Ivan is getting discouraged. He says it doesn't look like his college education has meant anything. He even hints at giving up the farm and taking a job again."

"Don't let him do that, Kate. You have too much here to leave behind. It is still my firm belief that two people in love and pulling together can accomplish just about anything – eventually. I had great hopes when we were married. I was in love, Kate, really in love. May Bell said she wanted a home and a couple of children. Then we'd travel together all over the United States and go abroad as we could afford it and my job permitted. Now I know she said that only because she knew that was what I wanted. After she got pregnant and we'd made the down payment on a house, an even better one than I could afford, her attitude changed completely. I honestly believe, Kate, it was her plan before we were even married to get a wedding ring, a baby and a house – then divorce me."

Kate was plainly shocked. She shook her head sadly.

"Those first few months, she played the part of the perfect little wife, sweet and loving. But as soon as she was sure she was pregnant, the change came. She began by moving me into a different bedroom 'just till the baby comes,' she said. I'd heard that women do strange things when they are pregnant, so I quietly put up with it and tried to be as understanding as I knew how to be. But after Sheila was born, matters only got worse. May Bell kept making big issues out of minor incidents and eventually she said it was no use: our marriage was not meant to be and the sooner we ended it the better. By then it was no blow to me. I had begun to see through her."

"I cannot imagine any woman, even May Bell, being that conniving."

"Kate, we lived for weeks in that house almost without speaking to each other. The only time she'd talk to me was when I was with Sheila; then it was 'Leave her alone, she's tired' or 'you're being too rough with her.' If I wanted to take her outdoors, the day was too damp or the sun too hot – always something. She'd put my meals on the table, what there was of them, then go to telephone or take care of the baby while I ate. Finally I gave up and spent as little time at home as possible. I just went home long enough to sleep – in my solitary cell."

Tears ran down Kate's cheeks. She had no idea it had been that bad. All this had happened to Tommy since last she saw him.

Tommy looked up from his elbows-on-knees position and saw how greatly Kate was moved. "Don't cry for me, Kate. The whole thing is my own damn fault. I shouldn't have troubled you with it."

"Oh, Tommy, it isn't a nice story, but I'm glad you told me. It brings us together again, and I was so afraid I'd lost you. She wiped away the tears and tried to think of something cheerful to say. "It's all behind you now, Tommy. Your best years are ahead. Relax and rest here away from it all as long as you can, then go on with your life and try to forget these past bitter years. You'll meet someone else soon and it will be the perfect marriage."

"Don't mention marriage again to *me*, now or ever. I drank too much gall in the first cup. I shall continue on as a middle-aged bachelor, going when and where I please, making friends with nice comfortable married people."

"Middle-aged!" Kate scoffed. "Tommy, for heaven's sake you're only 29."

"I feel a good 45. But I expect to drop off a few of those years soon." Tommy stretched and yawned, then smiled. "I feel better already. It's good to have you to talk to again, Kate. When is that lucky husband of yours due home?"

"He should be home any time now. Why don't you go to bed and not wait for him. You must be very tired after that long trip."

There was a little more small talk to end the evening cheerfully; then Tommy bid his sister good night and went upstairs to bed.

Kate remained on the couch going over the evening's conversation until she saw car lights coming down the lane. It would be Ivan.

He came in and sat down beside her but after a few brief remarks about the meeting, she sensed he had something else on his mind. He finally put it into words.

"While Tommy's here with you, I'm going to make a trip to the University, talk to Reed and some of those guys. See if they can tell me how to make more money on this farm this year. Wish you could come, too."

"Maybe under different circumstances, but not now, not even if Tommy weren't here. No. You go and find out how to make our fortune, then I'll go next time."

He added almost as an after thought, "So many muck farmers are turning to mint, but I'm not sure about it yet."

Ivan left right after chores Thursday morning. Bill was to do them that evening and the next day. He returned late Friday night after Tommy was in bed. Kate sat up eagerly waiting to hear what he had gained from the trip – if anything. She felt he wasn't anxious to tell her so she opened the conversation. "Was Mr. Reed still there?"

"Yes, he was there, but that isn't where I spent most of my time. Did you ever meet John Anderberg? He graduated in our class." Kate searched her memory, but couldn't place him.

"In lecture courses we usually ended up side by side because our names were next to each other alphabetically. But he was majoring in marketing. Well, he's with the University now doing market research. Reed sent me to him. We talked awhile, then he invited me out to dinner at their house last night. I stayed till almost midnight."

"And what did you decide?" In the back of her mind Kate was hoping just a little it was to give up farming. Maybe they'd even offered him a job.

"He convinced me to raise onions another year."

"Oh, no, Ivan. Is that all?"

"That's what I thought, too, but he put up a pretty convincing argument."

So it was all cut and dried that they were to struggle along for another year – and how many more – on those damned onions that hadn't brought them more than bare necessities.

"Here's the thing, honey," Ivan began the explanation, not sounding very confident. "He's been West recently, to that region of black soil where they raise onions with artificial irrigation. They are the farmers who have been giving the onion farmers here the rugged competition. Their early crop has frosted out this spring, and most of the farmers are replanting their ground with some other crop for this year. That means the onion buyers are going to depend on us again this fall. And since so many of the farmers in the muck belt here are turning to mint and potatoes, it might create a scarcity of onions like there hasn't been for a long time. You know what that will do to the price."

He paused and when Kate didn't comment, he continued. "I asked what he thought about mint, and he said he thought peppermint and spearmint were up and coming crops, but it would take a few years of uncertainty before the market is established for this community. He said it looked like it might be a good year to begin if I wanted to work my way into it. But, Kate, to begin mint there is a lot of different equipment I'd have to invest in. You start mint from the roots instead of seed. So if there is the prospect of a good year for onions ahead of us, I'm willing to tackle them for one more year."

"Do you think he knows what he's talking about? Farming is so unpredictable, how can anyone know what's going to happen?"

"Yes, I know, it's a gamble. But Anderberg must be pretty good or they wouldn't have him on the University staff." He paused again, then reached over and took her hand. "Honey, I promise you this. If this crop doesn't bring us a great deal more than what we've gotten any one of the last three years, we're giving up and getting out, 100-year-farm or no. I decided that on the way home. It isn't fair to you to keep up this struggle. Farms are beginning to sell again and our place has been improved enough, we could sell for a profit and settle wherever I can find a job."

It brought Kate some comfort to hear that something would happen at the end of one more season. It would make the hard scrabble through another summer a little easier.

"I also talked to Anderberg about my idea of marketing the smaller onions, those that fall through the screen and are thrown away." Ivan laughed. "His face lit up like a lamp and he said, 'Hey, you've got something there. Clean them up, pack them in 5 or 10 pound bags and sell 'em as gourmet onions.' "

CHAPTER 25

Sunday Dinner At The Rockwells

IT WAS PAST NINE O'CLOCK on a beautiful Saturday morning when Kate finally heard her brother stirring in the room above. She was glad he was beginning to relax and sleeping late. She pulled the black iron skillet to the front of the stove and placed a piece of home-cured ham in it.

Tommy sleepily entered the kitchen, carrying his shaving kit and greeted Kate cheerfully. "Do I have time to shave before that farm breakfast you keep fixing for me?"

"Go ahead. I won't put the eggs in yet."

Tommy finished shaving and returned to the kitchen where Kate had placed his breakfast on the table. He looked at the full plate and raised his hands in dismay. "You forgot the fried onions. Kate, you know I can't eat all that!"

"Eat what you can. I'm going to put some meat back on that lanky frame." She sat down opposite him with a cup of coffee. "How did you sleep?"

"Like an old mossy log in the forest. What wonders country living can do for a night's sleep. I didn't even hear Ivan come back."

"He came home late. And out again early this morning like every other day, summer and winter." She'd let Ivan tell about his visit to the University.

Tommy was examining a piece of toast. "How do you make these little brown squares on it?"

"Oh, I've learned a lot of things about country cooking – especially without electricity." She took down the round wire rack hanging by the stove. "After the fire burns down to embers, you take off a stove lid, open the draft so it doesn't smoke, then lay the bread on this little screen." She demonstrated. "Toast one side and then the other." She grinned at him. "See how clever I've become? I can even judge the temperature of the oven by putting my hand in it, like my experienced neighbor."

Tommy finished all but one egg and lighted his first cigarette. Baby Nan happily banged toys in the play corner of the kitchen. Eddie played with her for awhile then went to the low window sill and looked outside. He patted the window and began calling gleefully, "Shell-y! Shell-y."

Kate rose and looked out. "You're about to meet the first member of the Rockwell family. Here comes Shelly, bringing some baked offering, I'm sure." Kate waved to her. Michelle was just finishing her junior year in high school and had the prestige of being the oldest at home. Clara had married her Arnie and was pregnant. Mary was in nurses' training. Shelly finally had a room of her own with a heater she'd bought with money saved from weeding onions. Her father scoffed because it took so much electricity, but did not forbid it – at Serena's urging, Kate was sure.

"You'll like Shelly," Kate told Tommy. "She even reads poetry to me like you used to."

"Now, remember, when it comes to women, I've turned into a sedate old man."

"You can afford to like Shelly; she's only seventeen."

Eddie, who'd gone out to meet her, towed her across the front porch and into the kitchen. "Good morning." Shelly's eyes sparkled with the glow of spring; a belted pink dress revealed her slim young figure. "Eddie says you have somebody pretty important here." She glanced at Tommy, who had risen to his feet, and handed the pie to Kate.

Kate peeked under the cover, smiled a thank you, set the pie on the table and put an arm around Shelly. "This is Tommy, our long lost Tommy. Michelle Rockwell."

"Hello." She looked up at him with a smile.

"Bon jour, ma cheré, Michelle," Tommy greeted her with a slight bow.

Flushed and flattered, Shelly responded, "Am I supposed to call you Thomas or Tommy?"

" 'I hold he loves me the best who calls me Tom,' " he quoted, winking at Kate.

Shelly nodded. "From Thomas Heywood."

"Ah-ha, I see I don't need to sell her a set of encyclopedias."

"Parlez-vous francais?" Tommy asked.

"Un peu, Monsieur," Shelly shrugged.

"Come on you two Frenchmen, remember I didn't study the language," Kate interrupted.

"Actually, Mama sent me to invite you all for dinner tomorrow."

"Oh, that's an experience I wanted Tommy to have. Tell her thank you, we'll be there."

Baby Nan had crawled over to Shelly, who now picked her up. "Hello, sweetheart." She adored both of the children, as they did her.

"Go swing, Shell-y," Eddie begged, pulling at her skirt.

"All right, let's take Nan, too." She turned back to Kate and Tommy, "See you later."

When they had moved out of hearing, Kate said, "Isn't she sweet?"

"A very nice little girl." He stretched lazily. "Well, I'm going out to find Ivan and hear about his trip. Or shall I help with the dishes?"

"Heavens, no. Go on out into the April sunshine."

Just before one o'clock the next afternoon, Kate, Ivan, Tommy and the two children went up the lane to the Rockwell farm for Sunday dinner. Tommy exclaimed about everything in sight: the hay field, the bees, the butterflies, the birds, the maple trees just leafing out. It brought back the thrill Kate had experienced three years before.

Upon arriving, there were introductions all the way around, then the men settled in the spacious comfortable living room where several rag rugs were scattered upon the polished hardwood floor. An open stairway separated the parlor from the large dining room.

Kate went right to the kitchen to feed the children, Shelly helping, so they could be put down for naps before dinner. The beds were familiar to the children, since they were often at the Rockwells.

Clara and Arnie would be over later in the afternoon, but couldn't come for dinner, Serena said. Mary, looking fit and efficient, was home for the weekend from nurses training. Joe and Jimmy, just entering their teens, were completely involved in farming, fishing and basketball.

In the kitchen, Serena, as usual, was quietly making every minute count, removing baked chicken from a mammoth skillet and making gravy. Mary moved from one task to another, while Shelly was being told what to do: "Get the pickles and celery ready for the table. Put ice in the tea. Pour water."

Both girls seemed very aware of Tommy. Kate realized how suave and handsome he must appear to them. He sat in the easy chair closest to the dining room, seemingly more interested in what was going on there than listening to the farm-centered conversation in the living room. Rocky made a couple of polite attempts to get him into the conversation, asking about his job, the weather "out there," how long could he stay? But he soon wandered back to things in this community – his heartland.

Kate had warned Tommy that the Rockwells were a very conservative family. He'd better smoke outside, watch his language, and, "If you ask for a drink, you'll get water," she laughed.

"Oh, now, Kate, I think I can conduct myself properly around genteel people. But thanks for the tips."

When the call to dinner came and everyone moved toward the long white-spread table, Tommy gasped, "What a feast!" There was the huge platter of brown roasted chicken surrounded by oversized bowls of mashed potatoes, gravy, green beans, corn, coleslaw, homemade rolls and more. Shelly slipped up to the chair beside Tommy and he waited until she was seated before seating himself.

Mr. Rockwell asked the brief blessing and the meal began. Everyone but Shelly ate heartily. She took small servings, ate little and slowly. Several French words entered the conversation between Michelle and Tommy as they named the dishes going around.

Rocky spoke: "She learning the right words in that foreign language, is she, Tom? I couldn't tell, except what I see on her report card. She could be calling me all kinds of names and I wouldn't know it."

"Now, Daddy," Michelle scolded.

"All I know, she doesn't eat enough for a kitten." Her father smiled fondly and gently squeezed her arm as though testing her muscle.

Ivan sat next to Joe; they discussed basketball and the high school tournament. One of the first string boys had gotten hurt in a wood cutting accident and wasn't able to play.

"It reminds me of the story my uncles told about their escapade when they were sent out to cut wood. In fact they never told about it until Grandma died." Ivan shook his head. "If she had known about it, she'd have hit the roof for sure."

"What'd they do?" Jimmy asked.

"Uncle Jim said they'd take turns climbing up in a tall tree, then the others would cut it down so he could ride it to the ground."

There were exclamations of shock and amazement around the table, then Joe asked, "Can me and Jimmy do that, Dad?"

"Not unless you pick a tree no higher than your head."

"I guess even then boys had to get their jollies out of something," Kate said.

"What did you do, Dad?" Mary asked.

"We were kept too busy to get into much devilment. Except the time my brother and I tried to ride the old bull."

"How far did you get?" Ivan asked.

"About five feet and that animal was out of there and half way across the pasture field bawling like crazy."

"For goodness sake, Earnest, you might have been killed!" Serena exclaimed.

"Me? It was Clarence. I was standing behind the gate laughing my head off. I never did get my turn."

There was general merriment and other tales to tell around the table, then Serena and Mary got up to bring the dessert. Tommy patted his stomach and said, "I am stuffed!" but in German.

Shelly looked momentarily perplexed, then laughed. "That isn't fair. That's German or Norwegian or something."

Mary, bringing a large bowl of fruit Jello, said with an edge of exasperation, "Shelly, will you get more iced tea?"

None of the used dishes were removed from the table before dessert as was the custom in the community. Clean sauce dishes were passed around for the Jello and Serena brought in a beautiful hickory nut cake on a pedestal glass plate – three layers with nut filling and fluffy white frosting. It was Kate's favorite cake.

The meal over, Joe and Jimmy were soon shooting baskets into the hoop over the garage door. Rocky asked Tommy if he would like to see around the farm and the three men started out.

In the midst of the dish-doing by the women, Nan awakened and Shelly dropped her dish towel and hurried to get her. Kate picked up the towel and continued drying the dishes as Mary washed. Eddie had already awakened and went to join his daddy.

Shelly changed Nan, took her out to the front porch and sat with her in the wicker rocker. She began quoting nursery rhymes and acting them out, which brought delighted giggles from the baby.

Tommy heard them as he approached the house for a drink of water, after excusing himself from Ivan and Rocky who were deep in the controversy of onions versus mint. He hadn't smoked since arriving and was proud of himself.

Leaving the kitchen by way of the porch, he sat down in a chair next to Michelle and the baby. Looking out over the fields before them, he sighed contentedly. "Onion fields to the right and mint fields to the left."

"Some place to spend a vacation, isn't it?" Shelly remarked.

"Can you think of a better place?" Tommy turned and smiled at her.

"Well, yes. I'd choose a ski lodge in the mountains or a cottage by the sea . . . or maybe just a hotel room right off Central Park in New York City."

"I'm sure it's natural to want to visit places we've only read about." He watched the two of them: the baby patting her cheek and pulling at her long dark curly hair; Michelle fondling the plump little bare feet. He forced his gaze back to the fields. "Let's see, what verse do I know about onions?"

Michelle quipped, "How about, 'Eat no onions nor garlic, for we are to utter sweet breath'?"

Tommy laughed heartily. "Where did you come up with that one?"

"I looked up onion in Bartlett's Quotations. It's from Mid-Summer Night's Dream." After a pause she continued. "Did you ever teach school? You remind me of a schoolteacher."

"Is that good or bad?"

"Oh, good, of course. There should be more like you."

"No, I've never taught school. But frankly I have thought of teaching someday."

"Do you know what happened to my favorite teacher last year?" She looked very sober. "He was the best English teacher I ever had, like you, full of poetry and . . . and, well just nice, and had traveled a lot."

Expecting a tragic account, Tommy asked, "And what happened?"

"He was seen smoking in his car at noon and was fired. It just made me not want to go back to school . . . ever."

Mary joined them then. "Got out of dishes again, didn't you, little sister?" There was only a slight accusation in her voice. She sat down and Tommy began a conversation with her about nursing as a career.

Shelly left with the baby. "Let's go get Nancy a cookie."

At five o'clock Rocky and Ivan came in glowing from the fresh air and walk around their farms. "That ice cream ready to freeze, Rena? Ive and me can't do chores on an empty stomic." Serena said yes it was ready and went to get it.

To Kate's amusement, Tommy groaned good-naturedly. "You're not talking about more food!?!"

On the back porch, Rocky and Ivan took turns cranking the 2-1/2 gallon ice cream freezer packed with ice and salt and covered with a wet gunny sack.

Tommy, after offering his help, stood by watching, Kate beside him holding Nan. Later, when the turning got difficult Rocky called, "Mother, it's nearly ready."

Serena came, drying her hands on a towel. Shelly followed with pie pan and spoons. Kate was aware that Tommy was watching intently for the first peek, just as she had the first time.

The lid was carefully wiped and lifted, then Mrs. Rockwell slowly pulled out the dasher, scraping back into the can what she could of the creamy mixture. Joe and Jimmy's basketball went "thunk" into a corner as they grabbed spoons. On their haunches and holding the dasher over the pie pan, they dug in.

"Hey you two," their father said, "You didn't even turn the crank."

"No, but we had to milk out the cream," Joe said.

Eddie stood between them begging and received about every third bite.

"Want some?" Jimmy turned to Kate and Tommy.

"We'll wait," Kate laughed. "Three boys on that should just about finish it off."

Tommy was very aware of Shelly standing on the other side of him. Indicating the scene before them, he whispered, "Are you sure Norman Rockwell isn't lurking in your family somewhere?"

"No relation. And neither is James Witcomb Riley." They exchanged quiet laughter.

Serena brought Clara and her husband in for introductions. Tommy could see that Arnie was a born and bred farmer, large, rough hands, sun-burned face, hair combed flat back. Did Michelle have a boyfriend like that? He couldn't picture it.

Everyone received bowls of ice cream right from the freezer, as much in all the dishes as Rocky could persuade them to take. They then returned to the dining room, where the rest of the cake remained. A bottle of homemade strawberry syrup to go over the ice cream was brought in along with fresh coffee and iced tea.

Later, as they were saying their thanks and goodbyes, Kate noticed that Tommy continued to exchange witicisms and pleasantries with Shelly and seemed reluctant to leave. She knew he was having a good time with their sharp-witted little neighbor.

That night, Tommy lay pleasantly tired and thinking over his experiences here on the farm. The hurt left by May Bell was healing faster than he thought possible. How fortunate for Kate that she had come to this delightful place. He was sure their financial struggle would soon come to an end.

Then there was Michelle Rockwell. He sighed heavily. How could his attraction for this young girl be so over-powering!?! The impact of those big, blue eyes, fringed with inch-long lashes, left him mesmerized. Poetry . . . intelligence . . . compassion . . . humor – eat no onions nor garlic for we are to utter sweet breath. He laughed aloud. The baby patting her cheek. It must feel as velvety as a rose petal. He threw himself on his stomach and tried to sleep.

Up the lane at the Rockwell house, Michelle lay in misery, eyes wide open, staring into the darkness. Tears ran from the corners of her eyes and dripped on her hair and pillow. "Oh, God," she prayed, "don't let me fall in love again with a man I can never have."

CHAPTER 26

The Parting

RAPID STREAMS OF MILK hissed into the foam of the half-full pail as Ivan sat with his head buried in the flank of a cow halfway down the line. How long before he'd be able to afford a milking machine? Or a hired hand? He wouldn't think of getting either until Kate had her stove and refrigerator. His dreams of that first spring . . . Where had he failed? Or had he expected too much? By now he counted on having a large herd of Holsteins. Would all full-blooded cows assure them of a better income, or was it just a matter of pride? Rocky thought so and kept on with his nondescript herd of good producers. At the university, they hadn't talked much about dairying, just crops.

The windfall from Mattie had given him more high ground; but so far he hadn't been able to put things together to take full advantage of it. Fences had to be torn down and some of those buildings. But most of all, he needed a milk house with a cooling tank. And more help. It would be tough again this summer trying to decide what they'd have to have and what they could do without until fall and – hopefully – a bigger onion check. They had to be patient a little longer – poor Kate.

He hung the full pail on the hook by the wall and let the milked cow out of her stanchion.

Late that afternoon, Tommy returned with Ivan from a trip to Richland. Ivan went right to his chores and Tommy brought the groceries into the house, along with a box, which he handed to Kate.

"What's this?"

"Don't give up entirely making toast with the little brown squares, but that's for when you're in a hurry."

"Oh, Tommy, an electric toaster! How I've wanted one. You shouldn't have, but since you did, thank you!"

"It's small measure for all those meals you've prepared for me. Kate, do you know how much weight I've gained just since I came here? Five pounds! I spent a penny in town to get weighed. I've got to get out of here before you make a fat, bay-windowed man of me."

"Don't talk about leaving yet. You could easily take on another five pounds and be a long way from fat." His gradual return to the good old Tommy did not escape her watchful eye. He was eating more, smoking less and the old sparkle was returning to his eyes.

"No kidding, I do have to leave day after tomorrow. I called my boss from the telephone office. He's getting anxious for me to get to Pennsylvania. I can't live off my relatives in the lap of luxury forever. I've probably cost you a month of milk checks just to feed me."

"Nonsense, food comes cheap on the farm, as long as you're satisfied with the lack of variety. By the way," Kate added, "be sure to impress on Mother that you gained five pounds on my cooking."

"That's no joke. You've turned into a gourmet cook."

"It still isn't my favorite occupation, but you do what you have to do. So you might as well do it well."

"Practical Pat speaking again." He settled himself on a chair in the corner of the kitchen beside Eddie who was building roads with the wooden blocks he received for Christmas which Ivan had made. Nan sat nearby in her high-chair with the toy Kate had tied to it. Tommy made strange noises in his throat and played peek-a-boo with her, bringing delighted giggles. Kate realized he was enjoying them for themselves; they were no longer symbols of his own little Sheila who had been taken from him.

"Here's that grinder," Kate said mostly to herself. "I know Serena must be needing it."

"Want me to return it? I need the walk."

"Do you mind?"

"Not at all." Tommy got up, more eager to visit the Rockwells than he'd let on to Kate. He had seen Michelle for only brief periods since the Sunday dinner. Once she'd come down after school on some errand and saw him cleaning out the car, a cigarette in his mouth. She walked over to him, shaking her finger. "You scoundrel! Caught smoking! You shall be forever banned from the state of Indiana." He laughed, and had a wild desire to take her in his arms.

Another day he took a walk up the lane with Eddie just about the time he knew the school bus was due to drop off the Rockwell students. As they alighted he waved. All three waved back, then after a moment's hesitation, Shelly handed her books to Jimmy and came skipping over to meet them. She sat down on her heels, her skirt surrounding her, and hugged Eddie.

"Hey, don't Oncle Tom-mee get one of those, too?"

"Oncle Tom-mee's too big for hugs in the lane, isn't he, Eddie?"

Tommy went to the back door of the Rockwell house. He knocked, then opened it and called, "Hello."

Michelle was alone in the kitchen and turned from the sink where she was peeling potatoes. Her face brightened. "Hello!" she said, quickly dropping the potato and drying her hands.

"Kate sent this back with apologies for keeping it so long."

"That's all right. We haven't needed it." She took the small hand grinder, avoiding his eyes. "Mother and Dad went to Richland, the boys are doing the milking and I'm supposed to have supper ready by the time they get back. Sit down." She pulled out a kitchen chair.

"Thank you, I will, but go on with your work; I wouldn't want to be the cause of your not having supper ready on time."

Shelly went back to the potatoes. "I'll be headed for Pennsylvania day after tomorrow, Michelle, but I'll always remember this vacation. I had no idea Kate had moved to such a lovely place and among such delightful people. She's a millionaire and doesn't realize it."

"If it weren't for Kate, I think I would . . . suffocate." Shelly laughed to keep from sounding bitter, as she threw in the last potato, banged on the lid, set the pan on the stove and turned on the burner. "All the other people here talk about three hundred and sixty-five days a year are onions, cows and . . . food!" She laughed nervously again and sat down on the edge of the chair across from Tommy, clasping her hands together on the table in front of her and finally daring to look at him.

He smiled at her for a moment, then asked, "Are you going to college, Michelle? With that excellent school record, you surely should."

She looked down again and paused for a few seconds. "That's what Kate says, and my teachers. The folks expect me to go to college, too. I haven't had the nerve yet to tell them I want to wait awhile." Tommy said nothing, just sat quietly listening, so she hesitatingly continued: "I . . . I want so much to see some of the places I've only read about in books and . . . and dreamed of. Actually I'm sure I'd be a better student in college if I did get some of that out of my system first."

"That sounds pretty sensible to me. What would your folks think about it?"

"My father is very . . . strong minded. He'd think it's foolish and wouldn't pay for it; I'd have to do it on my own. And that's going to take a lot of onion weeding," she sighed.

"Yes, I'm sure it would." He wanted so much to encourage her. Even more he wanted to encourage her while holding her hands that lay between them. The long slender fingers would still be cold from the potato peeling. But he dare not side with her against family and teachers – even Kate. "Whatever you want after you graduate, I predict lady Fortune would have a hard time passing up. You know: 'Fortune leaves always some door open to come at a remedy'."

Shelly thought for a moment. "Shakespeare?"

"Don Quixote – Cervantes. Your potatoes are boiling. Am I keeping you too long?"

"Oh, no," she said quickly. She went to the stove and turned down the heat as she had so often been told to do. "There isn't much more to do but set the table. Mother knows better than to leave me with too much supper to get."

"Then if you have time, I'd like to see the collection of postcards you were telling me about. Maybe I can add to them."

"I'll get them, but they won't seem like much to you." She ran up the stairs to her room, looked in the mirror at her overbright eyes and flushed cheeks, pressed the back of her hand against her throbbing forehead, closed her eyes for a moment, then hurried back down, hoping her folks wouldn't come home or the boys wouldn't come in for just a few more minutes.

She spread the postcards on the table in front of Tommy. "I'm sure you've been to most of the places. I guess it's just the romantic sound of the faraway places that fascinates me. Whenever I hear of anyone I know taking a trip, I ask them to send me a postcard from some town with an unusual name."

Tommy smiled as he read: Santa Claus. Apple Creek. Valentine. Surrey.

"I'll see what I can find in Pennsylvania. But in return, you'll have to write me once in awhile about the happenings here in this place, which fascinates me so much. Kate will always know where to send my mail."

"I'll try to think of something to interest you," she said happily.

"I really must go now," he said, bundling the postcards together again. "Kate will be waiting supper on me."

"Won't you stay and eat with us?"

"No, thank you, Michelle, good as I know your supper will be. Kate is expecting me right back."

They were standing by the door. "Now do I get that hug I didn't get in the lane?" He sounded more beseeching than he intended. Shelly glanced quickly past him out the door and saw no one. She willingly stepped up to him and put her arms around his neck. All her sweet softness enveloped him as she touched her cheek against his. "Bon joir, Michelle, ma cheré amie. (Goodbye, my special friend.) Merci beaucoup."

He held her close for a few moments at the waist where her hips began to round and he could feel her body trembling. Then he released her and with one last loving look, he hurried away.

Shelly turned in a trance to the cupboard and automatically took out five plates and five glasses, the tears streaming down her face. Tommy, oh, Tommy, you'll be married to someone else when I see you again.

CHAPTER 27

Summer
1938

THE WEATHER WAS FAVORABLE for all crops during the growing season of 1938 in the muck region sometimes called "Long Swamp" which included the Stangland farm. Here is the heartland of America where geologists say that on one side of the road water flows to Lake Michigan and on the other side to the Gulf of Mexico.

Ivan had every possible spot of ground planted to onions. He was going for broke, he told Kate. Even the muck garden was smaller; so much of last fall's produce had to be hauled out in the spring and plowed under.

Most of the other farmers were busy working with a crop that was thus far unfamiliar to them. Growing peppermint was the main topic at every gathering where neighbors met, on the street corner or at farm meetings. Rocky was building a mint distillery, as were other farmers throughout the area. The harvest and distilling would come in late July or August.

Ivan was about the only farmer around still sticking with onions; he and a few unprosperous farmers too dogged to change, or poor families with enough children to do the weeding; pulling and topping themselves.

Kids to do such hand labor were getting harder and harder to hire; consequently the expense of labor took a large bite out of the onion farmer's profit. Most of the older boys were being hired for all-summer farm work. Others were working at resorts or national parks. Some were hired for part-time help setting pins at local bowling alleys. Girls were getting jobs as waitresses at nearby restaurants or serving as car hops for those offering curb service.

The labor problem added to Ivan's difficulty, keeping faith in a crop everyone else had given up on. He did manage, however, to locate a group of Mexicans who had come into this country and to a nearby community looking for work. They could speak very little English, but were dependable workers when Ivan showed them what to do. They were also thankful to be able to camp back by the lake, where they kept the area clean and neat. They often sang together in Spanish as they worked or in the evenings at the camp.

Kate, facing the fourth crop of onions, was skeptical but hopeful along with Ivan. She was afraid it would bring just enough more to keep them from leaving the farm, but not enough to do much with.

However on this August afternoon, all she had on her mind was to get down for a nap while the children were finally both asleep. Then she saw Shelly and her friend, Vera, coming down the lane. For once she hoped they were just taking a walk to the woods and not planning to stop. Shelly had come down alone several times, her eyes dancing with delight, when she received a postcard from Tommy. Kate knew they were meaning too much to her and she wrote as much to Tommy. He would be remembering her now as a nice little girl he'd promised to send postcards to. Yet impressionable Shelly, even with boyfriends her age, was clearly infatuated with Tommy.

Thankfully, the girls walked on by, chattering so fast they hardly looked toward the house.

Vera was saying, "Michelle Rockwell, you the best-looking girl in school and still mooning over that man almost old enough to be your father. The great Roy Grant all tied up in knots over you and you not caring if he ever asks you out again! Give him to me I'll be second fiddle!"

"You can have him. After last night he probably won't ask me for another date anyway. I was thinking so much about Tommy, I couldn't even let him kiss me goodnight."

"You know nothing can ever come of it, even if he does feel the same as you. Tell Kate, she'll talk you out of it in a hurry."

"I try to talk myself out of it," Shelly said near tears. "But you can't reason away being in love with someone. I dread the day Kate tells me he's engaged – or married. Now that the postcards have quit coming, I'm sure that's it anyway."

"Well, I suppose the man ran out of places to send them from."

"If I did get any more, Dad would probably write back himself and tell him a thing or two. You should have heard him when I got the last one."

"What did he say?"

"Oh . . . Jimmy brought in the mail and held up that postcard yelling,'Shelly got another card from her boyfriend!' Then Dad grabbed it and said, 'Stop that kind of talk.' He finally gave it to me – after he'd read it, of course."

"There wasn't anything revealing on it was there?"

"No, there never is. Just some clever remark or a line of poetry I'm supposed to guess. Believe me, if I don't recognize it, I find where it came from before I write back. But then I always have to sneak the letter out and mail it someplace else."

Ivan came in to supper, looking even more tired and haggard than usual from his long, hard days, trying to do the work of two men to keep from hiring more help. But he was, nevertheless, exuberant. "Gosh, Kate, those onions look good after we got them pulled. I bet it's the biggest onions, as well as the largest yield ever grown on this place – maybe even anyplace in Long Swamp. Rocky came by and said, 'Look at them suckers'," Ivan laughed.

Kate accepted the news with little joy. She was too tired to be excited about anything. The children woke up early and she didn't get her nap. Now she'd had to get up from the table several times to bring things she had forgotten, or wipe up spilled milk, or pick up what Nan threw overboard from her highchair. "Do you think they will bring enough to do much more than pay off the notes at the bank? The money you had to borrow to pay hired help."

"I sincerely hope a lot more. The market price is going up and I'm going to sack up those little buggers this year."

The Mexicans came back to top the onions from the windrows where they had been stacked after pulling. And a couple of them helped Ivan haul the full crates to the barn.

During the next few days of this heavy part of harvest, Ivan lay down to rest more than Kate had ever known him to do since they came to the farm. He'd come in at noon, eat only half his dinner with lots of iced tea, then lie down and fall instantly asleep, even with Eddie crawling over him. He'd finally wake up, take a couple of aspirin and go listlessly back to work.

"Ivan, you've got to take time off and get some rest," Kate insisted at noon on Friday.

"I am, I'm going to take the Mexicans back to Greenville tonight and let them have the weekend off." That evening he came in from his chores, ate a few bites of supper and dragged himself to bed. Kate was genuinely worried, but had so many other things to do before she could go to bed, she couldn't dwell on it. There were diapers to be brought from the line and folded, the children to bathe and the dishes to do. Why had she bothered to get supper? Hardly any of it was eaten.

When she finally got enough of her work done so she could go to bed, she was too worried to sleep. Ivan lay restlessly tossing beside her, even though apparently sleeping. He seemed feverish. Maybe she should wake him to take his temperature. But there wasn't much else she could do short of calling the doctor. If he were coming down with the flu or something, maybe she shouldn't be sleeping with him. She quietly got up, took her pillow to the davenport and soon dropped off to sleep.

In the early hours of the morning, loud panting sounds partially awakened her. She started towards the children's room, then realized it was Ivan awake, moaning and panting.

"Will you get me a drink of water?" he asked weakly.

Thoroughly frightened, she closed the door to the children's room, turned on the dresser light and got him the glass of water. Then she found the thermometer and took his temperature. It was 104°.

"I'm going to call the doctor," she said.

"No, not till morning anyway. Probably . . . flu . . . I'll shake it off."

He crowded into the covers with a chill. Kate brought a blanket, then stood over him, waiting and worrying. After the chill subsided, she went to the kitchen and warmed water to give him a sponge bath – against his protests. As she went over him with the wash cloth, she noticed red spots on his chest. What could they mean? She knew he had had chicken pox and measles as a child. Then her thoughts turned to a quarantine sign that hung on the front door of a house near Richland last spring. Serena Rockwell said someone there had scarlet fever. A couple of weeks later it was replaced with a black wreath of death. She shuddered and hesitated no longer to call Dr. Carter. He said she was taking proper care of Ivan and he'd come out first thing in the morning.

Ivan was asleep again, so she laid back down on the couch, but only to worry and pray. Except for a fitful few minutes, she didn't sleep again until daylight and time to get up.

The doctor arrived shortly after seven. She met him on the front porch and described Ivan's symptoms: the extreme fatigue, no appetite, headache, some coughing and now the red spots. He then went in, examined Ivan and returned to the kitchen with Kate.

"Has the well here ever been tested?"

"Not . . that I know of."

"You haven't been out camping or anything like that?"

"No . . ." Kate's throat tightened with fear.

"I don't know where he could have gotten it, but it looks like typhoid fever."

"Could . . . could it be the lake ice?"

"Are they still using that lake ice out here?" the doctor asked with a frown.

"Yes. A few of us. I've worried about it since I came, but no one else ever seemed to be concerned."

"I'm going to bring Dr. Mitchell with me as soon as we can get away this afternoon. He's had more experience with typhoid than I have. If it is typhoid, you should be immunized."

"Will we be quarantined?" she asked.

"No. That won't be necessary. But I'll bring you a list of precautions and the kind of care he needs. Have you been feeling all right?"

"Yes. Fine, just sleepy."

He patted her shoulder. "If it's typhoid, it's a mild case and he's young and strong."

After the doctor had gone, Kate sat down at the kitchen table and wept. She knew little about typhoid fever, but to her knowledge it was a long illness at best. The onions, oh, the onions. Whatever could she do about them? They would have to lay out in the field and get rained on, which Ivan said mustn't happen. The Mexicans were gone and she didn't know where. She couldn't communicate with them anyway to find out what they could or couldn't do. She'd have to get someone to do the chores right away this morning. It would have to be the Rockwells; if she called Bill, Ida was sure to come along and that was the last person Kate wanted to have around this morning. She couldn't call Rocky yet, though, or everyone on the line would be listening in at this time of day.

After feeding Nan, she put her back in the crib and hurried out to feed the chickens. When she returned, Eddie was up and talking to Nan through the bars of her crib. She helped him dress, gave him a quick breakfast and turned him out to the swing and sandbox. She'd have to call Rocky now.

"Why sure, the boys and me will do your chores," Rocky said after Shelly called him to the phone. "How did you get Ive flat on his back?" She told him what the doctor had suspected. He was thoroughly shocked and turned to relay the news to Serena.

At noon Dr. Carter returned, bringing with him Dr. Mitchell. It didn't take the older doctor long to agree that the diagnosis should be typhoid fever. The health department was notified to check on the other families who had been using the ice for table purposes and the little ice house would be forever closed against further storing of lake ice.

Kate set out some lunch for herself and Eddie and took Jello to Ivan, which he wouldn't eat. She realized she was so tired she was merely dragging her feet from one room to another.

Finally her family were all asleep and she could take a nap herself. But first she felt the need to get out and away from the house for a few minutes.

Not knowing where else to go, she walked slowly towards the barn. Soon it would be chore time again. Rocky said not to worry about them, but Kate knew they were busy with mint distilling.

The empty stacks of crates inside the barn again reminded her of the onions lying in the field. She fell on the nearest piece of machinery and wept, loud and unrelenting. A few days ago she had sighed bitterly over her faded dress and runover shoes. Now, real problems swirled around her like stinging hornets.

Was there some kind of hex on this farm? First Andrew and Susan. Then Tallock. Ivan's parents, too. "Is he the next?" she cried aloud. But she had to keep her senses and not give in to hysteria. The children and so much else depended on her.

She couldn't ask Rocky or Bill to go on doing their chores night and morning for the long time until Ivan was well enough to do them again. She could do nothing about the onions. There was no money to hire anything done. There was not even enough for groceries. And there was medicine to get. With what she found in Ivan's billfold after he paid the Mexicans, plus the change in her purse, it added up to less than five dollars. What could she do with that for a week? Katherine Patricia Morgan destitute! Fresh sobs of self-pity, tiredness and worry went through her. She could write her parents for money. They would send any sum immediately. In fact, they would be very upset if they knew she needed it so badly and didn't let them know. She wouldn't mind asking Tommy for a loan, he knew something of their situation, but where could she reach him immediately? And besides when Ivan found out, he'd never forgive her.

"What can I do? God, help me," she prayed, "I'm all alone with all this responsibility!"

She sobbed for a few moments, then her bleakness of spirit began to subside. She opened her eyes, and saw the green paint of the grain drill beneath her folded arms. The grain drill. The Easter eggs. The pennies! Where had she put them? When in her life had such a small sum seemed like a mountain of money? Not so many years ago she would have lightly spent that much on a pair of shoes. Now it would give them food and medicine for a few days. There. That was one problem solved already. Then she fervently prayed again, more calmly now, "Whatever I must endure during these next troublesome days, Lord, help me through it."

Kate hurried back to the house and found the heavy bag of pennies at the top of the kitchen cupboard. It would take courage to go to the bank to exchange them for larger cash, but pride must not stand in her way.

Now she must decide what to do abut the chores. Some way she'd have to get a hired hand; that all seemed clear now. With the utmost scrimping and letting the other bills go, maybe she could pay a man from the milk checks until they could get some of the onions sold. She had no doubt now they'd be selling the farm and leaving. Maybe Rocky could help her find a hired man. She looked in that direction and saw Shelly coming down the lane. As she entered the kitchen she said, "Mama thought maybe I could take care of things for you awhile so you can get some rest. Daddy said you'd been up most of the night."

"Bless you, Shelly," Kate sighed, "I'm about to drop."

"The children and Ivan are asleep, so I'll go upstairs and try to sleep awhile if I can. If Ivan needs me, or the children, don't hesitate to call me."

"I think I can manage, but I'll call if I need you."

CHAPTER 28

Merrick

AT FOUR O'CLOCK, Kate awakened, numb and aching. She couldn't immediately decide where she was or even what day it was. Then the clover wallpaper and the quiet voice of Shelly Rockwell downstairs brought time and circumstances into place. She put on her dress and shoes, knowing she must now go on with difficult decisions. As she appeared, Eddie hurried to her. "Shell-y here!"

Michelle, holding the book of nursery rhymes she'd given Eddie for Christmas, smiled up at her from the davenport. The house was tidy, the dishes done, little Nan played contentedly on the floor. Kate then peeked in at Ivan and found him asleep. "He woke up a couple of times, but didn't seem to want anything. I told him you were sleeping and he nodded his head."

"How in the world did you get all this work done in so short a time?" an amazed Kate asked.

"We did have to hurry, didn't we?" She hugged Eddie, sitting on her lap.

That evening after Shelly had gone and Rocky came to do the chores, Kate asked him if he'd help her find a hired man.

"Have you got money to pay one, Kate?" he asked frankly.

"I . . . I think I can manage for awhile, if we can find one who doesn't want too much."

"We're perfectly willing to do your chores, the boys and me, but I can see that Ivan would feel better about it if he had his own hand to depend on. Hard telling how long he'll be laid up. I'll inquire around tonight and tomorrow to see what I can find. But don't worry about the chores until we do find one."

The next morning Rocky reported that he'd found a fellow for her. He was the oldest of a large family who had recently moved into the community. Their small farm couldn't support all of them and the two oldest boys had to get out and look for work elsewhere.

"He's only nineteen, but always lived on a farm. Seems like a quiet, steady fellow," Rocky said of him. "He can come tonight if you want him."

Thus Merrick Osgood and his small cardboard box of belongings was dropped off at the Anderson farm by his father that Sunday afternoon. When Kate showed him upstairs where he was to sleep, he surveyed the neat, pretty room with double bed and was astonished. "You don't have to put me up in no style like this; I can sleep just anywhere."

Kate's heart reached out to this humble lad, who'd probably never had a room of his own before. She could tell him honestly their circumstances and he'd understand.

"With such a low salary, I want to give you the best board and room we've got. I don't know if Mr. Rockwell told you, but we can't really afford a hired hand. It's only that my husband is sick and we have to have someone to get the onions in so we can get them sold."

"I won't have to have no money for quite awhile," Merrick said earnestly, "If you give me my eats and don't mind my patched overalls."

His faith in her and his understanding deeply impressed Kate. Another thought occurred to her. "It will probably be pretty dull around here with just me and the kids. After the chores are done in the evenings or on Sundays, maybe you'd like to go fishing back at the lake. Ivan has poles in the barn."

His ruddy, homely face lighted up, but he hesitated a moment. "Golly, I'll get the work done up good and maybe I can go fishing." He looked as though any sort of recreation had never been a reward at his house, whether his work was "done up good" or not.

Before bedtime that evening, Kate discovered what a help the young Merrick was going to be in more ways than farm work. Ivan was too weak to lift much more than his arms. She called upon Merrick several times to help her with his physical care. He quietly, efficiently and without embarrassment did whatever was necessary, as though he were used to housework and helping with younger brothers and sisters. Ivan accepted his being there with only a brief explanation from Kate. He was too sick, his mind too hazy to care much about anything.

After Merrick was in bed, Kate sat down and again started to worry. If she could only help the boy get the rest of those onions in, or at least part of them before it rained. But how could she get away? Maybe they should just be scooped up and brought in under cover without being topped. She wouldn't know, she'd have to leave it up to Merrick. Ivan was too sick to make any decisions.

It would soon be time to fill silo again. Or would they fill this year? There was no doubt in her mind now that they would be moving. But it might be quite awhile before Ivan was up and able to look for a job and get the farm sold.

Well, she must not think any more about it now. Things always look bleaker at night. Faith and the morning might bring some solution.

By the middle of the week, Ivan's condition was somewhat improved, the doctor told Kate at the end of his visit. The fever was subsiding and he was more alert. As she sat at Ivan's bedside a few minutes after the doctor left, he asked in a weak voice, "What are you using for money?"

"Oh, I'm getting along just fine." She wouldn't bother him with any details or tell him about the pennies just yet.

Merrick had gone at the onions, topping as many as he could each day and bringing them into the barn each evening. But the job went slowly since he had to learn about the chores and do them before he could get out to the field. Then he must quit early to do them again.

Thursday morning, Ivan was aware of all that was going on around him, but then, as Kate feared, he began to worry. He went into such a depression that it was almost worse than the fever. The doctor had instructed Kate about Ivan's diet, but she'd found it almost impossible to get anything down him.

Friday morning she prepared a few soft foods and placed small portions on an attractive tray, then with a smile took his breakfast to him. But he turned his head when she entered the room and started to set it down.

"Take it away. I can't stand the sight of food."

"Ivan, you've got to eat or you won't ever get your strength back."

"Maybe later, but not now. Just take it away."

Kate returned with it to the kitchen, blinking back the tears. Why even try when he wouldn't cooperate? She'd had about all she could take, two small children and a farm to see to. But she couldn't give up now. "Give me strength," she prayed.

She had to find some way to cheer him up, get his mind off himself and their problems for awhile. She went in and turned on the radio, thinking that might help a little. No sooner had she got back to the kitchen then he called her again. "What did you say, dear?" she asked, going back to him.

"I said, shut off that damned radio."

Kate reached for the dial and realized the announcer was giving the weather forecast – rain by tonight or tomorrow. She could think of nothing cheerful to say, so she went back to washing dishes, tears streaming. If they hadn't listened to that darned John Anderberg, who'd probably never walked across a plowed field, they might have been raising peppermint and have it distilled and sold by now. The rest of the farmers had done all right for a first year. And all the Andersons had was most of a crop of onions waiting in the field to be rained on.

Hands in the dish water, Kate was so deep in her troubles she didn't hear the commotion in the lane until Eddie came shouting, "Mama! Mama! Look!"

She dried her hands and her eyes and went to the front door. Coming out of the Rockwell barnyard and down the lane was a procession of wagons, pulled by tractors and horses, two or three men to a wagon. "Good heavens," Kate murmured, "Are they going to fill our silo already without even telling us!" She watched dolefully, hanging on to Eddie.

They drove up near the barn, then left their tractors running, horses standing and came toward the house, grinning and playfully shoving each other like a bunch of mischievous school boys. When they neared the bedroom window, they burst noisily into song, completely off tune: "He's a jolly good fellow, he's a jolly good fellow, he's a jolly good fellow, Ivan Anderson! We'll top and screen them onions, them stinkin' old' yella' onions – for a great big chok'late cake."

The tears welled up in Kate's eyes again. When she reached Ivan, a trickle was running down his pasty white cheeks, also. She helped him rise to the window, where he waved a shaky hand to the laughing group of friends and neighbors, then fell wearily back to his pillow.

"God bless the neighbors," Kate sighed.

With trembling voice, Ivan said, "Now I know what that day of plowing for Fred Davis meant . . . to him last spring when he was laid up with a cast on his leg." He slid his hand to Kate's. "I'm sorry I've been such a grouch, honey . . . I feel like I've pushed the whole world over on top of you."

"Go right on being a bear, it proves to me you're getting better," Kate kissed him. "You've put up with me through two pregnancies, you know." She stood up. "Well, it looks like I've got cake to make."

"If you didn't feed that tray of food to the cats yet, bring it back. I'll try to eat some of it. It won't matter if it's cold. I'll have to force it down anyway."

Just as she reached the kitchen, the telephone rang. It was Serena Rockwell. "You got company down there?" she laughed.

"Oh, Serena, you'll never know what this means to us!"

"I have a good idea. I just called to tell you not to worry about their dinner. We're working on it now – Opal and Thelma and Ida. They brought things and the rest sent. Now don't give Earnest and me the credit for this, much as we'd like to have it. It was Ida got the idea and called the men. She's gone after the Mexicans now."

"Thank you all so very much. And tell the men their chocolate cake with ice cream will be ready for their break this afternoon."

After she hung up, she stood dumbly by the phone. Ida – good old giggling, interfering Ida Bryce.

Merrick came grinning into the kitchen. "They surprised you good, didn't they, Mrs. Anderson? I knew about it last night and I sure wanted to tell you this morning when Mr. Anderson was so upset, but they told me not to. I got to ask him now where his old onion screen is; they're going to set up another one."

CHAPTER 29

Nick Thaderus

THOMAS MORGAN, sitting in the one comfortable chair in his room, tossed the book he'd been trying to read across on the bed, picked up the pipe at his side, and stuffed it full. Why did thoughts of Michelle Rockwell have to interrupt everything he tried to do? After that hint from Kate to quit sending her the cards, he'd tried harder to give up thinking about her. He'd dated several other women nearer his own age, thinking that might help free his mind of her. But such evenings usually ended early. Each girl had seemed too much like May Bell and not enough like Michelle. There were times he'd gone miles out of his way, after studying the map, just to get another postmark to delight her – and to get a letter in return. Tom Morgan who was going to live the carefree bachelor's life, bound by thoughts of a seventeen-year-old high school girl who wrote fantastic letters.

After a summer of hard work, he had a ten-day leave earned. A couple of the fellows had asked him to go on a fishing trip with them, but he'd turned them down with a flimsy excuse. "You're going stale, Tom," Erwin had said. "Better change your mind." Yes, there was still time to change his mind. Maybe it would rid him of that haunting desire to spend time with Kate and Ivan. The country there this time of year must be beautiful. He thoroughly enjoyed his drives through the colorful Pennsylvania hills, but there were too few opportunities to get close to the trees, to be a part of the country side. He sighed. The Rockwells would be making applebutter outdoors in a big copper-lined iron kettle. There would be homemade bread to go with it . . . But he didn't dare go back there until he got over this foolishness about Michelle.

He puffed vigorously on his pipe for a few moments, then sprung to his feet. Jumping Jupiter! Maybe that would do it. The shock treatment. Go back there again, see her as she is, rather than the image I've built up of her. Get introduced to her adolescent, pimple-faced boyfriends. He paced the floor, rationalizing.

Driving right through, he could spend a few days there before heading back. He chuckled gleefully and sat down again. Damned if I won't do just that! Drive in and surprise them this time. Ivan is just getting over his bout with typhoid, maybe I can put in a hand here and there to help out. Poor Kate has had a rough year. Hope they can get a good price out of their onion crop this fall.

Kate and Ivan were desperately hoping the same thing. Now that the onions were in and ready to sell and Ivan up, at least part of each day, they watched the market nervously.

The crop had run almost seven hundred bushels to the acre. Possibly the best yield ever on the Stangland farm. To get them all to the barn, experienced neighbors with the help of the Mexicans, had filled and refilled the 18x15x12 inch crates that Ivan had made during the winters to replace those that were old and broken. Now the screened and ready-for-market fifty pound bags of onions were stacked in every available space on the main floor of the barn. Ivan didn't get a chance to try his marketing idea on the cull onions, but that was a small matter.

The price of onions kept sliding up a few cents with each report; but Ivan was worried that it might take an unexpected tumble. The few other farmers who'd raised any onions at all had already sold theirs. He received calls from buyers all over the Middlewest, who had someway heard about his onion crop. Each time he'd hesitate, almost ready to accept the high price quoted, then finally turn it down and go on waiting. He hadn't heard from Anderberg, after he assured Ivan he'd keep in touch.

One day Ivan put through a call to the University and when he got John Anderberg on the line, asked, "Shall I sell this big crop of onions?"

"No . . . Anderson . . . not yet. Hold them a little longer. I'll send a really good offer your way. And when it comes, you'll know it."

More waiting. The long distance calls from buyers slacked off, the market held steady, and Ivan became concerned again. Maybe Anderberg didn't know what he was doing with another man's crop. Maybe it was an experiment. They couldn't afford to go along with that.

At 3 o'clock on Wednesday afternoon, Kate answered the phone, then turned it over to Ivan when the operator asked for him. The connection was completed and the halting voice, heavily accented, began speaking: "This is Nick Thaderus . . . I buy . . . for Coney Islands. I talk to man from University . . . Anderberg. he say you honest man . . . have good onions. He say . . . if I offer you best price I can, now or later, he bet you sell to me. I give you t'ree dollars. Best price I offer now or later."

Ivan stood momentarily stunned. A hundred pounds of onions couldn't possibly be worth that much! "My onions are good, but I'd rather you'd see them. I'll hold the whole crop until you can come look at them."

"Good. Good. I be there sure tomorrow morning . . . late. Where do you live, exactly?"

Ivan gave the detailed directions, hung up the receiver and with color rising through his recent pallor, turned to Kate. "You'll never guess who wants our onions." She shook her head fearfully. He put his arms around her. "Coney Islands."

"Where you proposed to me!?!"

"The same. Only he's the purchasing agent for all of them." Ivan picked up a nearby pencil and figured on the corner of the newspaper. Then he showed Kate. "There, that's about what we'll get if Nick Thaderus takes them."

Kate gasped, then whispered. "Why, we'll be rich." After letting her imagination run wild for a few moments, she noticed that Ivan sat at the table and was gazing out the window as though his thoughts were far away. "What is it, my darling? Are you thinking of how the tide has finally turned?" Kate asked.

"Yes, in a way. But mostly I'm thinking of Grandma."

"Elizabeth?"

"Yes. Do you want to know about the first onions raised on this place?"

"Of course."

"Well, sometime in the early nineteen hundreds, a man came through here selling onion seed with the promise their company would buy the crop in the fall. After some consultation with her sons, she decided to go along with it and took enough seed for a couple of fields.

"It was a good year and the onions did well. As promised, the man came, or sent, I don't know which, for the whole crop.

"Time went by and the man came back with the check. No one was home so he came on in and laid the check under the sugar bowl here on the table.

"Later on Uncle Omar brought Grandma back from wherever they'd been. He went in the dining room or someplace and she happened to notice the check. Uncle Omar heard her cry out and hurried back to her. She sat here with the check in her hand, tears streaming down her face. She said to him, 'It's the most money I've ever seen at one time.'

"Onions have been raised on this farm ever since."

Kate and Ivan spent a restless night waiting for the next day to bring Mr. Thaderus. He arrived at 11 o'clock. Ivan met him as he drove in and walked with him to the barn, then opened a sack of onions at random and spilled out the contents on the barn floor.

Nick Thaderus got to his knees, examined them slowly and thoroughly, cut a couple of them open with his pocket knife, found them solid and white inside, then stood up. "I take them all. Coney Island got to have good onions. Plenty of good onions."

Ivan faced the short tawny-skinned Greek with the heavy dark brows beneath the graying hair, trying to think of more to say. He wanted to prolong this event he'd never forget. "I remember with a great deal of pleasure the times our family ate at Coney Island in Fort Wayne. We didn't get to the city but once or twice a year and that was the high point of the day for us kids, going to Coney Island." He decided against telling him about the proposal. "Have you been with Coney Island a long time?"

"Oh, yes, long time." He paused and grinned broadly. "I got kicked out back door too many times. Next time I come in front door."

Ivan laughed. "I guess that's about what's happened to us. We've been kicked out the back door the last few years. I just about gave up hope there was any front door for onions anymore."

The friendly purchasing agent looked up at Ivan as though sizing him up. "How about you raise onions for me each year? Eliminate the middle man, huh? I pay you good price."

Ivan shook his head slightly, "Well, I don't know, I'd almost decided to give up raising onions; but we'll see." Right now even raising onions for the rest of his life made him feel hilarious.

"Good. I keep in touch with you." He held out his hand. "My friends all call me Nick." They shook hands and walked back toward his car. "Oh, yes, I give you check now and balance when we get exact count." He put his foot on the running board and wrote the check, supporting the checkbook with his knee. After he had handed the check to Ivan, he winked at Eddie standing by looking intently at him. Drawing a handful of change from his pocket, he sorted out two quarters and pressed one in each of his hands. Eddie ran to show his mother.

"You come Chicago sometime, you call me up. We have hot dogs together, you and me, your wife and little kiddies."

"We'll do that. Thanks again," Ivan said with grateful sincerity.

After Thaderus drove away, Ivan went into the house and handed the check to Kate. "That is only part of it."

Tired from the excitement and walk to the barn and back, Ivan sat down at the table and leaned his head on his fist. "There is one thing I can't figure out. Why did John Anderberg go to so much trouble to sell my onions? He isn't the kind of fellow who'd expect anything out of it for himself."

"Maybe there's a catch to it yet," Kate said.

The next afternoon John and Louella Anderberg drove into the Anderson driveway. A surprised Ivan greeted them from the front porch and introduced them to Kate.

"We drove out to see a good onion farm," John said jovially. "How did you make out with Nick Thaderus?"

"Sold them all to him."

Later when the two women had gone into the house, Ivan and John sat talking on the front porch. Ivan said, "One thing I want to know. Why did you go to so much trouble to sell my onions, at a price way above my highest expectations?"

John laughed. "Part of my job, Anderson, part of my job. You pay taxes, don't you?" Then he looked away from Ivan out across the now-vacant muck fields. "No, you know that isn't it. For one thing I guess I was trying to prove I was right about raising onions this year. But even more, I'm just a frustrated muck farmer at a city desk. My parents lost their farm during the depression. Lost everything. It would have been too difficult for me to get back into farming again. Besides it wasn't much trouble to find Thaderus. I had a pretty good idea where they'd be needing onions, and needing them bad."

Kate and Ivan persuaded the Anderbergs to stay the night; Kate thoroughly enjoyed the vivacious Louella. She was Kate as she might have been if they hadn't moved to a farm. Not knowing what it was like to keep house without an electric stove or refrigerator, without a bathroom.

As they were leaving the next morning, John said, "You come visit us now, we'll re-visit the old U together. But make it soon, so we can visit you again."

CHAPTER 30

The Dress

MERRICK, THE BOY KATE HAD HIRED when Ivan was out of it all, was becoming invaluable. He learned fast and worked efficiently. Even though lacking in social graces, he was honest and polite. About as good a hand as could be found, Ivan decided, if he'd looked for one himself – even for more money.

How could he keep him through the winter so he would be there for the stepped-up production planned for spring? Maybe if Merrick were there to do the chores, Ivan reasoned, he could get away to go to the University more often and take advantage of those extra projects Professor Reed had mentioned: Doing some experiments and writing up bulletins. It might bring in enough extra to pay Merrick, as well as being the means to add more Holsteins to the herd. But he must move ahead wisely and cautiously; even a big onion check wouldn't last forever. He planned to plant a field to potatoes, those in the muck garden had done well. And he would plant onions for Thaderus, although not as many. He wanted enough diversification to eliminate some of the gamble.

Actually it was Merrick himself who came up with the solution. He had brought the last pails of milk to the back porch as Ivan was measuring and planning for the new milk house which would be built in part of the old woodshed. In the name of progress, the old dinner bell and the make-shift shower would come down. The new milk house would have a cooling tank, screens on the windows and a cement floor with a drain to hose it down.

Merrick came up behind Ivan. "Can I ask you something, Mr. Anderson?"

"Sure. What is it?"

"Well . . . me and my girl, Gertie, wants to . . . get married. And I was wonderin' if we could rent that little Enders' house cheap and fix it up a little."

"Married? Well how about that!" He reached out to shake Merrick's hand. "She seems like a nice girl." Ivan and Kate had met her once when she came and helped Merrick do the Sunday night chores. He went home between chore times on Sundays now since he'd bought a junk car and with the help of his brothers, got it running.

After a few moments thought, Ivan said, "Tell you what. If you two want to move into that place as it is now, tear down some of those fences and other trip trap, fix it up so it's liveable, you can have it along with your present salary. I'll give you meat when we butcher and milk as often as you need it. You can cut wood. Could you get along on that till spring when I'll raise your salary?"

"Oh, golly, Mr. Anderson, that would be hunky dory." The boy's ruddy face lighted up with a smile almost reaching his eyes. "Gertie's a good worker, too. She can be a cleanin' up that place while I work down here, then it will just be a hop, skip and a jump for me to go home." He was bouncing from one foot to the other. "Would it be all right if we went fishin' through the ice back on the lake sometimes? We sure do like ice fishin' and could bring you folks a mess when we're lucky."

"Sure enough. Should be lots of blue gills and bass back there." Ivan smiled fondly at the boy eager with anticipation, an emotion not foreign to the Stangland farm these days. Ivan clapped him on the shoulder. "You better get over and propose to Gertie right after chores this evening. We can set up the plan whenever you're ready."

Merrick nodded, still grinning, and loped back toward the barn. Ivan looked after him. He's a good kid and deserves a break. As for us, double luck! Not only do we have a hand for the winter, but the problem of what to do with Mattie's old place will be solved. He and Kate both hated to see it sitting there empty and dismal. They continually turned down offers to rent it; the little they would realize wasn't worth the risk of damage from unknown renters.

Ivan looked at his watch, then quickly stuffed the measuring tape into his pocket. He had promised Kate he'd be ready for the shopping trip to Fort Wayne by 10 o'clock. They were going to buy a new stove and a refrigerator and make a day of it since Shelly had the day off from school and could keep the children.

It was a beautiful autumn day after recent rains. The twenty-five mile trip to Fort Wayne went pleasantly as they discussed the new development concerning Merrick. Kate was overjoyed with the news.

"Maybe I can hire Gertie sometimes to care for the children when I have to leave them. Now that Shelly is a senior, I'm afraid she'll be too busy to keep them very often. And I do want to get out into the community a little more. They've asked me to work on redecorating the church basement. And the Home Economics Club wants me to work on the Christmas Tour of Homes."

"I'm glad you'll finally be able to do more things you want to do." Ivan took her hand and held it on his knee. "And I'm sure Gertie will be glad to earn a few extra dollars when Shelly can't keep them. She doesn't go out with boys much, does she? Surprising when she's such a good-looking girl."

"I hope it isn't because she has a continuing fascination for that brother of mine. He's probably charming half the women in Pennsylvania by now."

They parked in an all-day parking lot, then started out to compare prices and makes of stoves and refrigerators. They ended up choosing Sears for both appliances. After making arrangements for delivery, Ivan wandered over toward the milking machines.

"Are you going to buy one today?" Kate asked.

"No, I'm just curious. I'm going to wait for spring to invest in one. Then I'm going to my old boss in Chicago and see if he won't sell me one wholesale."

Kate could see that Ivan was getting very tired. She looked at her watch. "Is it time to eat yet? I'm starved."

Ivan's appetite had not returned, but for Kate's sake and on their special day, he wanted to go to a nice restaurant. "Let's go to the Hearthstone. It's close by."

Kate squeezed his arm. "Let's do, and pretend we're rich farmers."

He had waited to tell Kate over dinner about his idea to do extra work at the U. Kate was enthusiastic. "Maybe sometimes I can go with you when you have to make a trip in."

"I'm sure John and Louella would welcome us."

"Especially if we take them some potatoes and onions and squash and things. When I was growing up," Kate smiled remembering, "a cousin of my mother lived on a farm and they used to bring us things like that when they came to visit. I especially remember the cream. I thought a farm that produced all those things was some sort of wonderland."

Taking her hand across the table, Ivan said, "But this Alice wasn't in wonderland, was she? She had a nightmare."

"Oh, now, it hasn't been that bad. We've had our good times, too. We've weathered it together and are still in love . . . at least I am."

He squeezed her hand and whispered passionately, "Always."

"I guess Norwegian and Irish mix pretty well, huh?"

For dessert, Kate decided on pecan pie; Ivan ordered ice cream. As they waited for it, Kate said, "I'm so anxious to find out what we have to do to get our farm declared a one hundred year farm."

"Then I suppose we'll celebrate with a picnic," Ivan teased. He watched her face light up with ideas.

"Let's do have a party! A party for the whole community."

"A barn dance this time, I suppose," Ivan said, amused.

"I doubt if that would go over too well in our community. But we could have a neighborhood pot luck in the barn next spring after we are officially a hundred year farm. Maybe we could roast a pig, have balloons all up and down the lane, and dress in old fashioned clothes. You could wear Grandpa Tallock's wedding jacket."

"Oh, yes, I'd look swell in a tan linen jacket hanging almost to my knees."

"It was the latest style in his day. And I could take in one of Grandma Stangland's dresses to fit me."

Ivan sighed, "I'm sure there will be some happy ghosts present."

Kate began eating her pie. "I'm so happy about Merrick and Gertie. Mattie, bless her soul, would approve of them and their living there. I'll go up and help Gertie paper and fix up the place. I've been dying to get at it."

"When we buy paint for the barn we'll get enough to paint that house too," Ivan said.

"Yes, let's do. White, like the trim on the barn, with just a bit of green trim on the house."

Ivan laid his spoon down , leaving the rest of his ice cream as he had much of his dinner. "Now that we got the farm named, we can start painting the barn anytime."

"If you'll leave the high places to Merrick." Kate patted his hand.

After dinner, Ivan went to the car to rest. "Every afternoon till you get your strength back," the doctor had ordered. And Ivan was usually ready for those naps.

Kate had a long list of things to get, at least to look for, and Ivan told her not to hurry; it was her day. She finished with the most important on her list: a new coat for Eddie and some red flannel to make one for Nan. She smiled, remembering her resolution that hot day four years ago when she first realized she was pregnant with Eddie and envisioned a little girl in a red coat.

She also bought some pretty print for a house dress for herself, as well as some over-the-shoe boots. Deciding to be frivolous, she chose those with black fur around the top.

Returning to the car with two shopping bags full, she found Ivan asleep against the pillow they had brought along. She brushed his cheek with a kiss and said there were a few more things she wanted to look for. "No hurry," he murmured.

Unencumbered with the other packages, she went back to Wolf and Dessauers' department store to look for a dress-up dress for church and the holiday parties. It had been so long since she could buy a dress or even fit into a shapely one. Goodbye maternity dresses! At least for a few years.

She searched the racks and found a simple red dress which fit her well and could be dressed either up or down with jewelry, scarves etc. She decided on it, but on her way to pay, she was attracted to a dress on a model which stopped her short. It was in beautiful stunning black and spoke of true elegance. She gazed at it longingly, then checked the price tag. Horrors! But wouldn't she look great in that – dancy soft, self-fabric ruffles cascaded in tiers around the hem of the flaring skirt, shirred three-quarter length sleeves, wide black lace insert from neckline to shoulders.

After several moments of hesitation, she decided to try it on just to see what she looked like in it. Almost hoping she wouldn't find her size, she went to the rack beside the model. But there was a size twelve. Going back to the dressing room, she slipped it over her bare shoulders. It slithered down her figure like it had been custom made, even the length was perfect. All she needed was a pair of black suede spike heels. She just had to have that dress! It would mean doing without other things, but goodness knows she'd had practice at that.

I'll put it on lay-away though, she decided, not willing just yet to let Ivan know how much it cost. Someday she'd come back alone to pick it up and get some shoes and a black slip to go with it.

She dressed and carried it lovingly over to CREDIT LAY AWAY. The woman ahead of her was taking time with some complicated problem, so she glanced around the floor to other departments. Across the way curtains were displayed and she remembered how much she wanted new curtains before the stove and refrigerator were installed. She had wondered if they could afford them and here she was buying a dress three times what the red dress and the curtains would cost. Other thoughts reeled through her mind. Ivan's still-pale face against the pillow as he patiently waited for her, trusting that she would spend their money wisely. There were the doctor bills yet to pay. Ivan needed clothes too; he'd lost so much weight his pants hung from the belt. She had so much for herself already. They'd had such a pleasant day, one to be remembered, why spoil it with something she'd feel guilty over?

She slipped out of line, returned the black dress and took the red one. Maybe someday she could have a dress like that again, but not right now. Besides, where in their community could she wear it without feeling over-dressed? Perhaps once or twice the whole winter when they went to the University and out with the Anderbergs. Curtains were something she could see everyday and share with the family. Even Eddie noticed things like that.

Late that afternoon, Tom Morgan drove down the Anderson lane, parked his car in the yard and went quietly to the back door, opened it slightly and shouted, "Any old rags, old bottles or bones for sale?" Empty silence. Kate must be gone. No car around. Then he heard someone coming quickly through the house to the kitchen.

Michelle Rockwell stopped dead-still. "Tom!" she said weakly.

"I thought I was calling to Kate," he said dumbly, very much aware of a two-day beard and wrinkled clothes.

Her face was bright with joy. "Kate and Ivan aren't here right now. I'm keeping the children." She looked no younger, no different than his vision of her for the past three months.

CHAPTER 31

Rockwell Versus Rockwell

THE FOLLOWING MORNING Kate awaited the delivery of her beautiful new stove and refrigerator. She'd offer Gertie the little kerosene stove, which had served faithfully for four years, since there was no electricity yet in Mattie' s house. The old ice box with its despised drip pan forever running over, would be hauled to the junk pile. The freezer space in the refrigerator would permit Kate to bring home extra meat and vegetables from their frozen food locker in Richland. She could make ice cubes and keep ice cream, or freeze home-made ice cream in trays. The excitement of it all almost overpowered Tommy's visit.

Physically he looked well and seemed happy enough, but there was something on his mind he hadn't told her yet. Was he changing jobs? Or getting married again?

He had gotten up late after Ivan, with Eddie, had gone to haul a load of onions to the depot for shipping to Chicago. Merrick was loading and Ivan was driving them in.

As Kate gathered up the dishes from the breakfast table, Tommy sat absently playing the piano. Mattie's pieanna. Kate was determined to take piano lessons as soon as she found a suitable teacher. Her first piano lessons had ended somewhere around age twelve.

Tommy came into the kitchen finally, his cigarette finished, and picked up a towel to dry the dishes Kate had washed.

"Kate . . ." Tommy began miserably.

His unsuspecting sister laughed. "What or who is it this time? Tell all to your good old Aunt Polly."

"Well, get a good grip on the table, Aunt Polly. It's Michelle Rockwell."

Kate set a pile of plates down before she dropped them and looked at him in disbelief. "Oh, no, Tommy."

"I know . . . I know, Kate, what you're thinking. I've been telling myself the same thing, that it just can't be. Frankly, it is the biggest reason I made the trip back here this fall; to shock myself out of the vision I've had of her. But it didn't work. I'm beginning to think we were meant for each other in spite of the difference in ages."

Kate went on washing the dishes. What could she say? Finally she took a deep breath and began. "I almost wish you hadn't told me. I haven't any doubt but what Shelly is in love with you, or thinks she is. But you know what her parents would think about it." She paused, then finally continued, hating to say it, "You've got to work it out someway without involving Ivan and me, Tommy. Rocky and Serena have been like god-parents to us. I couldn't encourage this thing that would hurt them so much."

Seeing his crushed look as he set a dish on the table untouched by the towel, she quickly added, "They haven't anything against you personally, Tommy. But they expect Shelly to go on to college without marrying anyone yet." After another pause, Kate tried to add a lighter note. "Why couldn't you have fallen for her sister?" The thought of Tommy and the phlegmatic Mary made her smile even now.

"That's a nice practical suggestion," he said without humor. "I get the impression that that is what has been happening all along. The older girls and the younger boys get to do mostly what they want, but poor Michelle is constantly blocked from doing the kind of things she wants to do."

"Maybe that's because Mary and Clara and the boys fit in better with the plans their parents had for them."

"Is it such a sin to be different!?! To follow one's own beckonings, rather than that of your parents?"

"*I* don't think so, Tommy, but I'm not her parent."

"I'm sorry, Kate. I realize you aren't responsible for any of this. You even tried to do what you could to stop it when you saw what was going on. But it was too late. I think now, I fell in love with her the first time I met her. I tried not to think it, to crush any such feeling, but I've finally given up." After a long look out the window at the Rockwell house and a deep sigh, he continued, "I wish I knew what there is about the girl that has me mesmerized. It isn't just her beauty, lots of girls are beautiful. Even May Bell was – on the outside. But Michelle is mature, intelligent, witty, full of romance and poetry, compassionate . . . How does a man explain why he has fallen in love? Especially after being such a damn fool the first time."

"Don't compare Shelly to May Bell. I guess I dare say that you and Shelly, except for age, are as compatible as two people could be. But you see, don't you, why I can't encourage any togetherness here? That whatever takes place between you must be at Rockwells – not here?"

Still looking out of the window, he did not answer. Kate's heart went out to him. "I'm sorry, Tommy, really, really sorry. I think so much of both you and Shelly. I wish there were some way to convince her parents, peacefully. After all, who's the salesman around here? Not me."

Tommy finally turned from the window and with hands in his pockets, said, "Maybe I can, Kate. Just maybe I can. If only I were sure Michelle is old enough to know I'm really what she wants. After a whole summer you'd think one of us would have lost interest if it wasn't meant to be."

The next evening after Tommy had spent the day helping with the onion-hauling, he put his head in at the Rockwell's back door and found Earnie and Serena and Shelly in the kitchen.

"Come in stranger. Heard you were back again," was Rocky's hearty greeting as he looked up from shelling the small ears of popcorn with his gloved hands. As he rubbed one small ear against the other, the dry sharp grains fell into a large pan.

Tommy returned the greeting and spoke to Mrs. Rockwell and Michelle, then held up three tickets. "A boy at the depot this morning sold me tickets to a band concert in Richland tonight. I thought maybe Kate and Ivan might want to go, but they were both too tired. So I thought I could interest somebody here."

"May I go, Mama?" Shelly asked eagerly. Serena glanced at her husband.

"All three of you go," Tommy said, "we'll get another ticket."

"I'm about ready for bed myself. You want to go, Mama?"

"Oh, I don't care much about band concerts, but I guess Shelly can go if she wants to."

"Well, jump into your duds then, child. Don't keep him waiting," Rocky said to his daughter.

Shelly dropped the dish towel and ran up the stairs, took out her best dress, then put it back. No, she wouldn't do anything to make this look like a real date with Tommy. She put on her favorite school outfit, a flared black wool skirt and plain white blouse with bright blue tie at the neck. Just a little lipstick. When she returned to the kitchen carrying her school jacket, Tommy was just finishing the dishes she'd left. He looked deep into her eyes and smiled. She cautiously smiled back.

The band concert was of little interest to the pair who sat close together talking in a corner of the pavilion. It was mostly impersonal, but the joy of being together with parental consent heightened each remark, each look, each nudge, as the band played one piece after another.

With the excuse they would beat the crowd to the Sweet Shop, the two left early by a side door. After their refreshments, they returned to the car. He unlocked the door for Shelly, then went to the other side and got in, but didn't start the car. He turned to her, elbow on steering wheel, and looked at her for a moment before speaking. "Michelle, do you know about me?"

She answered without hesitation, "Do you mean that you've been married and divorced and have a little girl?"

"Yes . . . I guess that's what I mean." He looked past her at the dark street outside. "Also that I'm two years older than Kate."

"I know. Kate told me all that before I ever met you."

"And you don't hold all those strikes against me?"

"No, not at all." She paused, looking down and rolling the corners of her scarf. "Only that . . . after I'd met you . . . I just couldn't see why any woman . . . would want to leave you."

"Oh . . . my darling." Tommy took her softly in his arms. Kissing her was the ecstasy he knew it would be. "There isn't another girl like you anywhere. No other I can even think about," he murmured, still holding her close, his cheek against hers. "I love you, Michelle. I want to marry you."

"Tom, oh, Tom, I love you too, and want so much to marry you . . . and never, never be separated from you again." They clung together and their hearts beat wildly.

"There is only one thing, Tommy," she said, pulling herself gently away from him, "You've no idea what my parents would think of this . . . if they knew. They have no objection to you; they just wouldn't think I'm old enough and they would object to the difference in our ages."

"I do know, Michelle. I see them refusing to believe you've grown up. I'm going to try to convince them that we can surmount that difference. I may be bodily thrown off the place, but after the initial shock, perhaps they will see how it is with us. I wouldn't want to take you away from your parents without their consent, but I'm willing to wait, Michelle, until you can speak for yourself."

"I'm willing to wait, too, Tommy." She paused now, twisting the school ring on her finger. "You know, ever since I was a little girl and can first remember, it seemed like I was waiting for something, or somebody, somewhere. I didn't know what it was, it just gave me a sad, heavy feeling. Then when I first met you, I knew. It was almost as though . . . I'd grown up just for you. I even learned to like my name after you spoke it."

Without words, Tommy took her in his arms again, held her hard and firmly. Oh, God, what kind of wonderful creature is this? "I'm going to talk to your father tomorrow. This mustn't go on without their knowing it. I'll see just how much he does disapprove."

"No, Tommy," she said pulling herself away again. "I'll talk to them first. They won't throw me out. If Daddy goes through the roof, you'd better stay away a day or two, then you can try."

"Tell me something," Shelly said on the way home, "Who sold you those concert tickets when you had to pay at the door, too?"

Tommy groaned. "Now you're going to find out I'm a liar, also. Well, I saw the announcement about the concert on a billboard in Richland. And I found those old raffle tickets in my billfold."

"I knew no one was out selling tickets to that band concert. And you knew darn well my folks wouldn't go to one if they were. What a wily salesman you are."

"I expect that to be the last lie I ever tell them – but I was desperate." She laid her head on his shoulder and the bond between them was golden.

The next day was Saturday. Tommy went directly after breakfast to his car parked in front of the house and pretended to clean its interior. He had spent a sleepless night after telling Kate only that he'd taken Michelle to a band concert with her parents' consent. He watched the Rockwell farm closely, ignoring Eddie's chatter as best he could until the boy finally grew tired of being ignored and went back in the house.

After the usual going back and forth from house to barn at chore time, Tommy saw the Rockwell boys with their fish poles coming down the lane. They invited him to go fishing with them; he politely declined. If there had been any sort of announcement at home yet, they said nothing about it. Then he saw Mrs. Rockwell leave in the car; Michelle had said her mother was going to be busy at some kind of food sale. Now Michelle was alone with her dad. Would she tell him or wait for her mother to come back?

He felt so damned weak and tongue-tied leaving it up to her. Maybe in spite of what she'd said, he should go up there now. He nervously smoked one cigarette after another, trying to make up his mind. Then he saw a slim figure in a blue dress come running out of the house and toward the lane. Oh, my darling, Michelle . . . what has happened!?! He threw down his cigarette and went to meet her, fear and a feeling of finality with every step.

Michelle, too, had spent a sleepless night, planning her strategy, just what she would say. She urged her mother off early, volunteering to do the morning work after she left. Then Shelly waited for the first opportunity to talk to her father; she was determined to get it over as soon as possible.

She washed the dishes and started sweeping the kitchen floor. Now she saw her father coming in with the mail. He silently sat down at the kitchen table, checked the letters, then started looking at the paper. When she saw him turn from the front page, she began, "Daddy . . ."

"Uh, huh."

"I'm seventeen. Clara was only eighteen when she got married."

Earnie Rockwell looked up from the farm market report. "Now don't tell me you're getting the notion. I thought that Grant feller was coming around a little too often all summer," he said, frowning.

"It isn't Roy Grant, Daddy. It's Tommy Morgan." Shelly held on to the broom and looked at the floor, waiting breathlessly for the explosion. When she heard nothing, she lifted her eyes. Rockwell looked at Rockwell. He grinned.

"Girl, for the first time in my life, I see the Rockwell sticking out all over you." He paused and gazed at her. "You can't bake a pie without help; you still have to be told to wash dishes; you're all but afraid of a cow; but here you are telling me something that you knew was enough to make me blow up. Something I'd have had to find out through Mother if it had been either of the other girls. Is this just your idea or is it his, too?"

"Just last night we discovered how much we are in love. I promise you, Daddy, it's the first time he's ever kissed me . . . but we've been in love since last spring. He said it mustn't go on without you and Mama knowing about it. He wanted to come to you, but I said I'd talk to you first."

"Your Mama and I haven't been blind to this," Earnie Rockwell said solemnly as he fingered the corners of the paper. "We've suspected you wouldn't end up a farmer's wife. You didn't seem much interested in going to college either. When those postcards came from the city fellow, I saw how eaten up by them you were. I thought maybe it would pass, but I guess it hasn't, not so far, at least." He looked up again, studying her.

"There was fifteen years difference between your Grandma and Grandpa Rockwell. She married young and they had a good long life. If he's the right man, might be it'd work out for you, too." He pushed away the paper. "Well, Shell, we'll see. You've got another winter of school yet; you go ahead and graduate. If by spring, you both feel the same as you do now, you can speak for yourself. If you can't cook him a decent meal, maybe he can afford to hire a cook and have you to look at."

Michelle dropped the broom with a bang, went to her father and hugged him tightly, "Oh, Daddy, Daddy, you're the best father in the whole wide world. I'll show you this winter that I can cook and keep house. I've always thought it no use to try. Clara and Mary were so much better than me. You all thought I was such a child. And I'll graduate, too, maybe even at the top of my class. I haven't told you that, yet, and I may even go to college, eventually, even though I'm married. But for awhile, I just want to read, read, read – and travel with Tommy."

Rocky patted the daughter on his knee with pride and fondness. He had never understood this third child, but was proud to have sired such a beautiful and brilliant daughter. She was like a princess in his family. "You know, girl, you remind me of a heifer I used to have," he chuckled. "Lady, I called her. She'd always walk around the mud instead of plodding through it. She'd stand up and bawl all night before she'd lay down in a wet pen. But you know that temperamental critter turned out to be one of the best producers I ever had."

Michelle laughed, her eyes shining. She was too rapturously happy to be disconcerted by the comparison to a cow.

"Now, we'll have a real surprise for Mama when she comes home, won't we, you and me?" He spanked her lightly on the backside. "Better run down to your book peddler and tell him the news. He's been hanging around out front watching. And tell him to put in a little more time around here. Maybe we can even teach him to milk a cow before he leaves again."

At the foot of the lane, Michelle leaped into Tom Morgan's arms and sobbed out the joyful news. "It's all right . . . Daddy knew it all along . . . I just have to graduate first."

It took a moment for Tommy to comprehend, then he said, "Michelle . . . Michelle, this is absolutely the happiest, most sublime moment of my life. We'll fly to every horizon and be together always."

Kate stood watching from the kitchen window, attracted there by Shelly's quick trip down the lane. She dared to be happy for them now. Evidently somebody had sold somebody something, maybe even a number of things. She saw them turn and walk hand in hand up the lane as Eddie from behind her called, "Mama, what's this?" He was carrying her bundle of knitting.

"Oh, honey, don't pull out the needles. That's Mama's . . . crazy quilt," she said absently, her mind still on Tommy and Shelly. Since the first weeks of their marriage she had been working on the afghan by fits and starts. Like Mattie at her piano, if she were perturbed over something she'd knit like crazy. On long winter evenings while she and Ivan listened to the radio, she'd knit leisurely. Then again busy months would go by and she wouldn't touch it.

Eddie still stood looking at her with questioning face, so she smilingly spread it over the kitchen table to show him. She stood back and looked at it in perspective. The pattern wasn't crazy, it was attractive and harmonious. The ebony black of the muck fields, the green of the woods and the onion tops in summer. Gold and crimson for the flowers and autumn leaves, white for the snow-covered lake, just as she intended. She pointed them out to Eddie.

"Now Mama will add some gray rows for when Daddy was sick and we all felt so sad. Then it will be . . . all done!"

He laid his cheek against it. "Ain't it soft?"

For once she didn't correct him. "You little rube," she said, tipping his face to meet her loving gaze, his eyes the blue of Ivan's.

"What's a rude?"

"A rube? Oh, that's a boy who doesn't like to be anyplace but in the country."

"Is Daddy a rube, too?"

Kate laughed. "Yes, Daddy's a rube, too."

"Daddy said he's going to put my name on the barn when he paints it."

Kate went to the window framed by the new canary-yellow curtains and looked out on the farmyard – their campus – a silo, hog pens and chicken houses surrounding the barn. Had Susan, Libby and Nan, in their time, looked out from a kitchen window on this place and loved it as I do, Kate wondered.

She pulled Eddie's curly brown head to her side. "Won't our farm look grand? All those buildings painted red and white, then over the big barn door the name: ONION AVENUE. And under that, IVAN ANDERSON AND SON.

"Why we going to call it Onion 'Ven-u?"

"Because onions have been grown on this farm for a long, long time, Eddie." She patted her cheek. "Maybe you'll be raising onions here someday."

"Why?"

Kate sighed. "Well, I guess because God seems to want us to grow onions on this farm."

After a pause, Kate said, "Do you know, Eddie, we're going to have a big birthday party for our farm next spring? About the time you're four years old, the farm will be one hundred years old. Eddie's eyes opened wide. "Can little kids come to the party?"

"Of course. Little kids, big kids . . . everybody."

"Even God?"

Kate smiled. "Yes, God for sure."

"Can I go out and play in the sandbox with my new tractor?"

"Why don't you do that. Then when Nan wakes up we'll all go up the lane after the mail."

Eddie went skip-hopping out the door and Kate sat down at the white oil-cloth-covered kitchen table to enjoy a few minutes of fulfillment. Homey, happy sounds surrounded her: the quiet hum of her new refrigerator; Nan's awakening; Jenny wren's final aria before leaving for the southland; and Ivan's merry whistle from somewhere around the barn.

EPILOGUE

THE 160-ACRE STANGLAND FARM no longer raises onions; nor do any farms in the area. However a former street festival has been revived in the little village of Wolf Lake and Onion Days is held each year in mid-August.

Danny Stangland, the great great grandson of Andrew (who came from Norway in 1824) presently operates the farm and like his great grandfather, Tallock, teaches school.

A grandson of Tallock's, Jay Stangland, at 85 cultivates 2-1/2 acres of blueberries on another plot of Andrew's original farm and has taken off as many as 2,000 pounds of berries in one day.

Andrew and Susan's direct descendants number in the hundreds. Many have been or are farmers with a fair sprinkling of schoolteachers as well.

Andrew and Susan Stangland, Tallock and Elizabeth and many of their descendants are buried in the Merriam Christian Chapel cemetery just off route U.S. 33, where a red bird often sings of the past and of the future.